NORSE POEMS

ATHLONE
LONDON

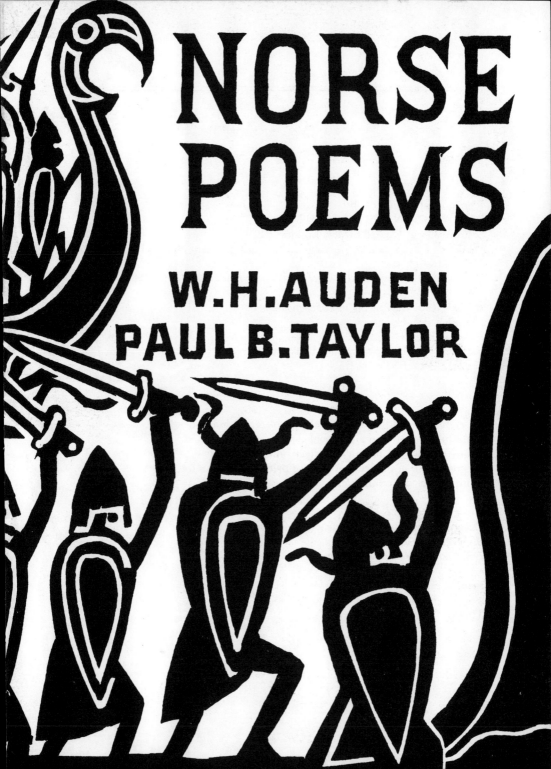

NORSE POEMS

W. H. AUDEN
PAUL B. TAYLOR

First published in 1981 by
THE ATHLONE PRESS LIMITED
at 90-91 Great Russell Street, London WC1

© Paul B. Taylor and The Estate of W. H. Auden 1969 and 1981

British Library Cataloguing in Publication Data
  Auden, W. H.
  Norse Poems
  I. Title   II. Taylor, Paul Beekman
  821'.912   PS3501.U55N

ISBN 0-485-11226-4

Designed by Jim Reader
Design and production in association with
Book Production Consultants,
7 Brooklands Avenue, Cambridge

Printed in Great Britain by
The Thetford Press Ltd.
Thetford, Norfolk

Contents

Part III The Mythological Poems

Acknowledgements

"The Lay of Völund," "The Waking of Angantyr," "The Treachery of Asmund," "The Lay of Erik," "Brunhild's Hel-Ride," "The Words of the High One," "Skirnir's Ride," "The Lay of Harbard," "The Lay of Hymir," "Loki's Flyting," "The Lay of Thrym," "The Words of the All-Wise," "The Lay of Vafthrudnir," "The Lay of Grimnir," "Baldur's Dreams," and "Song of the Sybil," copyright 1967, 1968, 1969 by Paul B. Taylor and W. H. Auden, appeared in *The Elder Edda* (Faber and Faber and Random House, 1969).

Requests to quote from or reprint any of the contents of this volume should be addressed to Faber & Faber, London.

For

Kristján Eldjárn, former President of Iceland
and for Iceland herself in her second millennium
of democracy

Foreword

The poems in this volume are to Iceland what the works of Hesiod and Homer are to Greece. They are the repository of national myths and legends. Yet, they are much more, for in time they have become the heritage of myth and legend for all the Germanic peoples. What we know today of Norse mythology and heroic legend comes ultimately from this traditonal material, from the stories of Odin's wanderings, Loki's deceptions, and Thor's battles to the legends of Sigurd, Brunhild, Gunnar, and Attila the Hun. W. H. Auden's interest in these poems began with his Oxford reading, and with his early experiments in verse forms, was heightened during the visit he and Louis MacNeice made to Iceland in the thirties, and was renewed when he revisited Iceland in 1965. It was after this last visit that he decided to collaborate on a version in English of all the important early Icelandic traditional poetry. It is a poetry whose metrical line is difficult to capture in modern English verse, but Auden has maintained the alliteration and the strong stress quality of Icelandic. Where he felt English verse forms could not adequately represent the rhythm of the Icelandic line, he turned his source into a syncopated prose.

This poetry was written down in Icelandic in the thirteenth century, although earlier versions may have existed, for some of the poems, as early as the tenth century. Some of the poetic references to nature describe Norwegian landscape, and at least one poem, *The Greenland Lay of Atli*, was composed in Greenland, and it mentions polar bears and describes a trip across an icy fjord. Most of the poems in this collection were preserved in a single manuscript which an Icelandic Bishop, Brynjolfur Sveinsson, presented as a gift to the King of Denmark in 1662. In the late nineteen sixties it was returned to Iceland by the Danish people in recognition of Iceland's recent independence from Denmark.

The English text attempts to preserve as much of the quality of Icelandic names as possible without being unnecessarily pedantic. Proper names are usually retained in Icelandic spelling, although some names whose meaning seems pertinent to the context are transformed into English. So, when Sigurd disguises himself behind the name *Gofukt Dyr*, the name is rendered as "Noble Beast." Some names are normalized into modern Icelandic form, especially in places where the verse calls for a two-syllable name. Old Icelandic *Baldr* is, therefore, rendered *Baldur*, while *Egill* is shortened to *Egil*. The Icelandic alphabet is reduced to a modern English form, except for the retention of the umlaut mark over *o* , where it is to be pronounced as the *o* in English *word*.

My debts in preparing this collection on behalf of Auden, are many. Hérmann Pálsson of Edinburgh and Hreinn Benediktsson of Reykjavik encouraged the initial undertaking. Peter Foote of University College, London, advised the inclusion of "The Sun Song". Thordur Einarsson, Jóhann Hannesson, and Einar Benediktsson offered continual encouragement. The National Translation Centre, Austin, Texas, provided me with a travel grant to consult with translators of Icelandic. Maurice Taylor corrected the final typed copy and collated it with the Icelandic text. I owe a special debt to Peter Salus, friend of Auden's, who was a go-between Auden and myself while Auden was in New York and I was in Switzerland. He ordered the materials, prepared a type-script and was unstinting in his suggestions, notes, and comments. Edward Mendelson, Auden's literary executor, has provided valu-able advice and information, and Brian Southam, of The Athlone Press, has shaped this material into its final form. My deepest debt is, of course, to Auden himself. No collaboration could have been easier. He knew the material so well that he rarely had to check obscure points with me. He went to the Icelandic itself. I gave him my translations in the best poetic line I could manage, and he turned that verbal and metrical disarray into poetic garb. The product is his. I am glad to have had a role in providing a raw material.

There are seven places in the text where I or Peter Salus supplied missing material, indicated in the text by brackets:

"The Lay of Atli"—Strophes 23 and 24 were missed by Auden (undoubtedly because of the similarities in formulaic diction). The present text is my original supplied to Auden.

"Gudrun's Inciting"—Strophe 21 was missed by Auden and is supplied from my draft version.

"The Lay of Hamdir"—Strophe 22 (a notorious crux) Auden mistook the Icelandic hrod-glöd "glad-of-fame" as a reference to Gudrun (some editors place this strophe after strophe 10 to enforce this point). If the strophe is left in its proper place according to the manuscript, the speaker has to be a woman in Jörmunrek's court who warns the brothers, rather than their mother, who is not at the scene. So, I had to change Auden's line to make the strophe relevant to its context. His line read:

Gudrun heard them and answered thus—

stood listening, slender fingered—

Your lives are in peril if you pay me no heed, *etc*

"The Words of the High One"—strophe 107 Auden missed the fifth line. My draft version is used.

Strophe 153: The last line was missed by Auden and supplied by P. H. Salus.

"The Song of Rig"—The last line of strophe 36, and the last line of strophe 41 were missed by Auden, and are supplied from my draft.

"The Lay of Harbard"—Strophe 16, line 2 was missed by Auden, and supplied by me.

P.B.T.

Glossary

Aegir's daughters	waves
ben	mound
blood-worm	sword
bane of fell dwellers	killer of giants (Thor)
din-world	mortal world, world of pain
dis (plural disir)	natural spirit
elf-candle	sun
Flame-of-the-Rhine	gold
Gleams-of-dread	gold
Hel	Norse land of the dead, similar to the classical Underworld
howe	cairn, burial mound
kolga's sisters	waves
sark	coat of mail
tree-foe	fire
Thing	Council, Parliament
Thurse	giant, primordial being
weregild	the compensation to be paid for killing a man

Part I

The Viking Poems

The Lay of Völund

Nidud was the name of a king in Sweden. He had two sons and a daughter. She was called Bödvild. There were three brothers, sons of a king of the Finns. One was named Slagfid, the second Egil, and the third Völund. They ski'd and hunted beasts. They came to Wolfdale and made themselves a house. There was a lake called Wolfsea. Early one morning they found three women spinning flax on the shore. Near them were their swan-cloaks. They were valkyries. Two of them were daughters of King Hlöder, Swanwhite Hladgud and All-Wise Hervor; the third was Ölrun, daughter of Kjar of Gaul. The brothers took the maidens home with them to their hut. Egil took Ölrun, Slagfid took Swanwhite, and Völund All-Wise. They stayed seven winters. Then they flew away to seek battles and did not come again. So Egil ski'd out to find Ölrun, and Slagfid sought Swanwhite. But Völund sat in Wolfdale. He was the most cunning of men, as we know from the old lore. King Nidud had him taken by force, as is told here in the poem.

> Three maidens through Mirkwood flew,
> Fair and young, fate to endure:
> Winged maidens by the water's edge
> Peacefully retted precious flax.

> Ölrun was the first; she took Egil for lover.
> Swanwhite the second; she took Slagfid.
> Hervor the third; she threw round Völund's
> White neck wanton arms.

> So they sat for seven winters,
> Then in the eighth for home they longed,
> In the ninth their dooms drove them apart:
> Three maidens through Mirkwood flew,
> Fair and young, fate to endure.

> The weather-wise hunters, Egil, Slagfid,
> Returned from the hunt. The hall was silent:
> They searched all about but could see no one.

East after Ölrun Egil rode,
South after Swanwhite Slagfid,
But Völund sat in Wolfdale alone.

Red rings he forged, enriched them with jewels,
Rings he threaded upon ropes of bast,
Faithfully waiting for the fair-haired
Hervor to return to his hearth-side.

When the Lord of the Njars, Nidud, heard
That Völund sat in Wolfdale alone,
He sent warriors forth: white their shield-bosses
In the waning moon, and their mail glittered.

They drew rein when they got to the gabled hall,
In they came through the end door,
Rings they saw, on ropes threaded:
Seven hundred, all owned by Völund.

These they unthreaded, but there they left them,
All but one, just one they took.
Then the weather-wise hunter, Völund, came
On light feet back from a long road.

He piled up logs, prepared for roasting
A brown bear: well burned the fire
Of wind-dried wood before Völund's eyes.

The lord of the elves lay on a bear-skin,
Counting his rings; a red one he missed:
He deemed in his mind that the daughter of Hlödver,
Hervor, had returned to his hearth-side.

Long he sat till asleep he fell;
What he knew when he woke was not joy:
He saw on his hands heavy chains,
His feet in fetters were fast bound.

"Who are the men who my hands have chained?
Who have fettered my feet together?"

Then the lord of the Njars, Nidud, answered:
"What good have you gotten, greatest of elves,
From our treasure, Völund, in Wolfdale?"

Then said Völund:

"Was there not gold on Grani's Road?
Far thought I our realm from the Rhine hills.
Greater treasure we had in olden days,
At home in the hall, happy together,
Hladgud and Hervor, Hlödver's children,
And wise-counselling Ölrun, Kjar's daughter."

Nidud the king gave his daughter, Bödvild, the gold ring he had
taken from the bast at Völund's. And he himself wore the sword
which had been Völund's.

Without stood the wily one, wife of Nidud,
In she came through the end door,
Stood there smiling and softly whispered:
"Woeful shall he be who from the wood comes."

He gnashes his teeth when he notices the sword,
And on Bödvild's arm beholds his ring,
His eyes glare, grim as a snake's:
With a knife they cut his knee-sinews,
Set him on the island of Saevarstöd.

There he fashioned all sorts of precious things for the king. And no
man except the king dared to voyage thither.

"From Nidud's hip there hangs a sword,
The blade I sharpened with a sure eye,
The blade I tempered with a true hand;
Now the shining steel is stolen from me:
Back to my smithy it shall be born yet.

"Bitterest to bear, bitterest to behold,
Bödvild wearing my wife's ring."

Fierce, unsleeping, at his forge he hammered,
Making for Nidud marvellous things:
He saw two boys, the sons of Nidud,
At the door of his smithy on Saevarstöd.

They beheld a chest, they asked for a key.
Evil was on them as in they looked.
There were gems in plenty, precious stones,
And red gold to gladden their eyes.

"Come to-morrow, but come alone.
Gold and gems I will give you both.
Tell not the maidens, tell not the courtiers,
Let no one know of our next meeting."

So they returned, the two brothers,
Said to each other: "Let us see the rings."
They beheld a chest, they asked for a key.
Evil was on them as in they looked.

He struck off the heads of those stalwart boys,
Under soot-blackened bellows their bodies hid,
From both their skulls he scraped the hair
And set them in silver as a sight for Nidud.

Of their eyes he fashioned excellent gems
For his dear neighbour, Nidud's wife,
And out of the teeth which were in their mouths
He forged a brooch to bring Bödvild joy.

Precious beyond all price to Bödvild
Was the ring she had broken; she brought it to Völund:
"None but you are to know of this."

"Mend it I can so the marred gold
Shall appear to your father fairer still,
In your mother's eyes look much much better,
'While to you it will seem the same as before."

Ale he brought her, the artful smith:
Long they sat till asleep she fell.
"Now all but one for my hurts are paid,
All but the most evil of women.

"I wish that my knees be well again,
My limbs that were maimed by the men of Nidud."
Laughing rose Völund, aloft in the air,
Weeping fled Bödvild, away from the isle,
Afraid of her lover and her father's wrath.

Without stood the wily one, wife of Nidud,
In she came through the end door.
The lord of the Njars lay there resting:
"Nidud, husband, are you awake?"

"Awake am I ever and without joy,
Little I sleep since my sons are gone,
Cold is my head, cold were your whisperings,
Now with Völund I wish to speak.

"Learn me, Völund, lord of the elves:
Where are my boys? What has befallen them?"

"Oaths first shall you all swear me,
By ship's keel, by shield's rim,
By stallion's shoulder, by steel's edge,
That you will not harm the wife of Völund
Nor cause the death of his dear bride,
Who shall in the hall bring up our child.

"Go to my forge which your folly built,
There find the bellows blood-bespattered.
I struck off the heads of your stalwart boys,
Under soot-blackened bellows their bodies hid,

"From both their skulls I scraped the hair
And set them in silver as a sight for Nidud,
Of their eyes I fashioned excellent gems
For my dear neighbour, Nidud's wife,

"And out of the teeth which were in their mouths
I forged a brooch to bring Bödvild joy,
Bödvild who goes now great with child,
Your only daughter, dear to you both."

"Never have words brought woe more bitter.
For vengeance, Völund, in vain must I long.
No man is so tall to take you from your horse,
No sharp-eyed archer can shoot you down,
There where you hang, high in the clouds."

Laughing, Völund rose aloft in the air:
Sorrowing, Nidud sat there after.

"Thakrad, best of thralls, go quickly,
Go to Bödvild, the bright-browed maiden,
Bid her come forth; her father awaits her.

"Is it true, Bödvild, as I am told it is,
That you and Völund, when you visited him
On the lone island, lay together?"

"It is true, Nidud, as you were told it was.
Völund and I, when I visited him
On the lone island, lay together.
A day of ill-omen, an hour of sin.
Against his wiles I had no wit to struggle,
Against his will I did not want to struggle."

The First Lay of Helgi, Hunding's Killer

In olden times when eagles screamed,
Dropped holy waters from Heaven's fells:
Then was Helgi, the huge-hearted
Born in Bralund to Borghild.

Night had fallen when the Norns came,
Those who appoint a prince's days:
His fate, they foretold, was fame among men,
To be thought the best of brave kings.

There in Bralund's broad courts
They spun the threads of his special doom:
They stretched out strings of gold,
Fastened them under the hall of the moon.

They hid the ends to east and west:
All the lands between belonged to the prince.
One to the North Neri's sister
Drew and ordered to hold forever.

There was one who harmed the Ylfings' son,
And the maiden, too, who mothered him.
From a high tree one hungry raven
Cried to another: "I know something."

"One day old, wearing his byrnie,
Stands Sigmund's son; he will soon be renowned.
His glance is trenchant like a tried warrior,
A friend of the wolf. So we shall feast."

The household thought him an heir of Dag,
Declared that good days had come upon men.
From the din of combat then came the king,
Bringing his son a beautiful leek.

Helgi he named him, Hringstead he gave him,
Sunfell, Snowfell, and Sigarsvellir,
Hringstead, Hatun, and Heaven's plain:
For his brother Sinfjötli a blood-worm was made.

So he grew to manhood among friends,
A high-born elm, an idol of fortune:
Rings and gold he gave his follower,
Out of his blood-bespattered hoard.

Sigmund's son was soon ready
To wage war: fifteen winters he had
When he slew Hunding, the hardy warrior,
Who long had ruled over lands and thanes.

For that Hunding's heirs demanded
Bright rings from the boar-helmed,
Payment in full for their father's death,
A recompense for their plundered lands.

The prince said he would pay nothing,
No weregild at all to Hunding's kinsmen:
He threatened them with thunderstorms
Odin's anger and ashen spears.

The chieftain journeyed to Logafell,
Sigmund's son to a sword-meeting.
Frodi's peace was broken; the bitches of Vidrir
Roamed the isle, eager for corpses.

The hero sat under Eagle Rock:
By him had Alf and Eyjolf been slain,
With Hjörvard and Havard, Hunding's sons,
The whole family of fierce spear-wielders.

A light blazed on Logafell,
And flames flashed forth from that light.
They stood under helmets on Heaven's Plain;
Their bright byrnies were blood-bespattered,
And sparks flew from their spear-points.

Soon the prince asked the southern maidens
If they would come home with them,
From Wolfwood as warriors' brides
That very night: there was noise of battle.

But from her horse Högni's daughter
Stilled the shield-clatter and said to the prince:
"I think that I have other business
Than drinking beer with the dealer-of-rings.

"My father has pledged me, promised his daughter
As bride to Granmar's grim son.
But Hödbrod, Helgi, I have called to his face
A king as valiant as a cat's son.

"He will come to fetch me in a few nights
Unless you face him on the field of slaughter,
Or take me away in time from the warrior.

"Have no fear of Isung's killer:
It is death now for him or death for me."

Over air and sea the all-wielder
Sent a messenger then to demand a host,
To offer heroes and heroes' sons
Great abundance of gleams-of-dread.

"Bid them quickly equip their ships
And sail out to battle from Brand-isle."
The prince awaited the war-eager
From Hedin's island, hundreds of men.

Ships outfitted with shining gold
Struck out towards him from Stafnsness:
Helgi asked Hjörleif this:
"Have you mustered the men we need?"

Hjörleif answered Helgi thus:
"To tally the ships from Trönu's beaches,
The long-beaked ships, laden with warriors,
And to row out into Örvasund
In battle-trim will take long.

"We have twelve hundred trusty men,
But in Hatun the host of the king
Is larger by half: we are in for a battle."

Then the steersman struck the prow-tents
And woke the warriors, the war-eager;
The sons of Dag for daybreak watched;
The mast was hoisted by the men of the king,
And the woven sails in Varinsfirth.

Oars splashed, iron clattered,
Vikings rowed, rands clashed;
Far from the shore the foaming sea
Flew by under the fleet of the king.

When the long keels and Kolga's sisters
Came together the clash sounded
Like a sea storming a stern cliff.

Helgi ordered them to heighten the mainsail,
In those vessels there were no waves of cowards,
Though Aegir's daughters did their best
To sink the sea-steeds and send them Hel-ward.

But Sigrun from above saved them all,
The brave ones in their beaked ships:
The beast-of-sea-din was safely kept
From the grip of Ran in Gnipa's wood.

In the evening at Unavagur
The fair-decked fleet floated at anchor,
But battle-rage arose in their hearts
When they saw the army from Svarinshill.

Then Gudmund spoke, the god-born:
"Who is the leader at the head of these troops
Who ferries to land such a fierce host?"

Sinfjötli slung to the sailyard then
His red shield, rimmed with gold:
Sinfjötli there was the sound-warder,
The knower-of-answers, and answered thus:

"Say when you feed your swine this evening
And order your bitches to eat their swill,
That the Ylfings are gathered from Gnipa's wood,
Have come from the east, eager for war.

"There will Hödbrod find Helgi the prince
In the midst of his fleet, flight-unwilling,
Who often gave eagles their fill
While you dallied at the querns with dairy-maids."

"Little you heed old tales
When you tell such lies to true men,
You who have eaten the offal of wolves,
Your brother's bane, a beast who often
Cupped wounds with cold mouth
And lurked in caverns, loathsome to men."

"You were a witch on Varin's isle,
A fox-wise woman who fashioned lies.
No man, you said, should mate with you,
No warrior except Sinfjötli.

"You were vile, an ogress, a valkyrie,
Peevish and hateful to All-Father.
Valhalla's heroes must all battle
To please your fancy, fickle woman!

"Nine were the wolves that we had
At Saganess: I sired them all."

"You were no father to Fenris-wolf,
Though you are older than all I remember,
For Thurse maidens at Thorsness
Near Gnipa's wood had gelded you.

"You were Siggeir's stepson and slept beneath house-posts,
Were accustomed to wolf-songs in the woods outside:
Treachery was natural to a nature like yours,
When you cut out the heart of your own brother
And made your name for monstrous deeds."

"You were Grani's bride at Bravellir,
Gold-bitted, agog for the race:
You were slender under the saddle, hag,
In those days when I rode you downhill.

"You looked like a low-born slut
When you milked Gullnir's goats by yourself,
And uglier still as Imth's daughter
In a ragged dress. Would you wrangle longer?"

"Sooner would I sate ravens
With your dead flesh at Frekastein
Than lead your bitches to lap their swill
Or feed your hogs. Let fiends revile you!"

"It would be better for you both, Sinfjötli,
To go to war and gladden eagles
Than to do nothing but duel with words.

"The sons of Granmar are not good to behold,
But truth becomes a king's speech:
They have made it clear on Moinsheim
That they have the heart to handle swords."

They gave rein and rode with speed,
Svipud and Svegjud to Solheim,
Through dales bedewed and dark woods:
The sea-of-valkyries shook as they rode.

They came to the armed-one at the court gate,
Stridently cried: "The stillers are coming."
Without stood Hödbrod, helmet-crowned,
Watching the ride of his war-eager kinsmen:
"Why have the Hniflungs such angry faces?"

"Keels turn hither, heading for the beach,
Big-masted, with bellying sails,
With many shields and shaved oars,
Glad Ylfings, the host of the king.

"Fifteen thousand have ferried to land,
In Sogn, as too, there are seven thousand,
Blue-black long-ships inlaid with gold,
Gathered in the harbour near Gnipa's wood.
Most of his army are here now.
Helgi is set for the sword-meeting."

"Let the bitted steeds ride to the battle of kings,
Sporvitnir to Sparinsheath,
Melnir and Mylnir to Mirkwood,
And let no man remain behind,
None who can wield a wound-flame.

"Invite Högni and Hring's sons,
Atli and Yngvi and Alf the Grey,
The brave warriors, war-eager:
The fierce Völsungs shall feel our anger."

In one sweeping movement they met in battle
On the field of spears at Frekastein:
Ever was Helgi, Hunding's slayer,
First among men where the fighting was;
War-eager, unwilling to flee,
The folk-defender showed a fearless heart.

Then from overhead came the helmeted ones
To guard the king. There was clash of spears;
Wound-givers flew; the wolf ate
The raven's food; Sigrun cried:

"Hail leader and luck-bringer!
Kin of Yngvi, be happy now.
The foe has fallen, felled by you,
Boar-helmeted, bringer-of-death.

"To-day you have gained a double prize,
A mighty maiden and much treasure.
Hail, king! Hold and enjoy
Both Högni's daughter and Hringstead,
Fame and land. The fight is won."

The Lay of Helgi, Hjörvard's Son

There was once a king named Hjörvard, who had three wives. The first was called Alfhild and their son Hedin; the second was called Saereid and their son Humlung; the third was called Sinrjod and their son Hymling. King Hjörvard, who had sworn a solemn vow to take as a fourth wife the fairest woman on earth, heard that King Svafnir had a daughter, called Sigrlin, who was fairer than all other women.

Hjörvard's earl was named Idmund. He had a son called Atli. One day Atli was standing in a certain grove when he saw a bird perched on a branch overhead. It was heard that men called Hjörvard's women the most beautiful of all. The bird chirped and Atli listened to what it said.

"Have you seen Sigrlin, Svafnir's daughter,
The fairest of maidens in Munarheim,
Fairer even than Hjörvard's wives
Who gladden men's eyes in Glasir's wood?"

"Wise bird, I beg you to speak
Further with Atli, Idmund's son."

"I will if Hjörvard offers me sacrifice
And grants me whatever gift I ask for."

"You must not ask for Hjörvard or his sons
Nor for any woman wedded to the king.
Nor for the beautiful brides of his men:
Let us come to an agreement as good friends should."

"I will ask for a temple with timbered altars,
And gilded-horned cows from the king's stock,
On the day when Sigrlin sleeps in his arms
And embraces him of her own free will."

Hjörvard sent Atli to visit King Svafnir and ask for Sigrlin's hand. He stayed all winter in Svafnir's court. Svafnir had an earl called Franmar. He was Sigrlin's foster-father and had a daughter named Alof. Franmar advised Svafnir to deny Hjörvard's request, so Atli returned home. Hjörvard asked him what tidings he brought. Atli answered:

> "I have troubles to tell of; my tidings are bad.
> Our horses met hardships in the high fells,
> And we had to wade through the waters of Saemorn.
> Then Svafnir refused us, on Franmar's advice,
> Sigrlin his daughter, endowed with rings."

Hjörvald told Atli to go a second time, and he himself came with him. When they reached the summit of the fells and looked down on Svavaland, it was in flames and a great cloud of dust hung over it. They descended and stayed the night by a river. Atli kept watch and crossed over the river. There he came to a house. On its roof, guarding it, sat an eagle, but the bird was asleep. Atli killed it with his spear and entered the house. There he found Svafnir's daughter Sigrlin and Franmar's daughter Alof. The eagle he had killed was really Franmar who by sorcery had changed his shape.

There was a king named Hrodmar, who was one of Sigrlin's suitors. It was he who had killed Svafnir and plundered and burnt his land. King Hjörvard took Sigrlin, and Atli took Alof.

Sigrlin bore Hjörvard a son. He was tall and handsome and of a quiet disposition. No name stuck to him. One day he was sitting on a mound when nine valkyries came riding past, one of whom was more beautiful than all the others. Her name was Svava, and she was the daughter of King Eylimi. She said:

> "Early, Helgi, an eagle screamed:
> You will rule rings and Rödulsvellir
> In days to come if you keep silent
> Until you are ready to wreak revenge."

> "What plans for my future, fair maiden,
> Giver of orders, have you in mind?
> I will never take the name "Helgi"
> Unless I may have you: answer me truly."

"I know of swords in Sigarsholm,
Four fewer than five tens:
Among these weapons one is the best,
A gold-wrought blade, a bale to armour."

"A ring is in the hilt, a heart at mid-blade,
Terror in the point when it pierces foes,
Along the blade lies a blood-stained serpent,
And a coiled adder above the guard."

Then Helgi came to his father and said:

"You were ill-advised, Hjörvard, I think,
Famed though you be as a battle-leader,
When you let the land be looted and burned
Of a king who had never caused you harm.

"That is why Hrodmar holds the rings
Which before our family held:
Life-secure, that leader sits,
And intends to keep the treasure of the dead."

Hjörvard replied that he would give Helgi a host of warriors if he
would avenge his mother's father. Helgi went to Sigarsholm to find
the sword Svava had told him of. Then he and Atli went forth and
slew Hrodmar and did many deeds of valour. Helgi also slew the
giant Hati as he sat on a mountain top. Hati had a daughter named
Hrimgerd. One night, when Helgi and Atli lay aboard ship in
Hati's firth, and Atli was keeping the first watch, Hrimgerd
approached and said:

"Who are the heroes in Hati's firth
    In ships decked with shields?
Wolfish you look as if little afrights you:
    By what name is your king called?"

Atli said:

"He is named Helgi: you never can
    Hope to do him harm.
His ships are surrounded by shields of iron:
    No wishes can work against us."

"Mighty warrior what is your name?
   What do your kinsmen call you?
The leader must trust you if he lets you keep
   Watch over his war-fleet.''

"'Atli'" to men, 'Menace' to you,
   A terror to troll-maidens:
At a wet prow I have watched often
   And hewn night-riding hags.''

"Corpse-greedy wolf-tail, what are you called?
   Who was your father, witch?
Forty miles deep is your due home,
   While barley sprouts from your bosom.''

"Hrimgerd my name, Hati my father's,
   First and fiercest of giants:
He carried off many a maiden from her home
   Till Helgi hewed him down.''

"It was you who lay under the hero's ships
   Before the mouth of the firth,
Would have given Ran his glorious warriors
   If his spear had not spitted your flesh.''

"Over your lashes you have let your brows
   Droop in a dream, Atli.
That was my mother: by me, though, Hlödvard's
   Sons were drenched in the sea.

"You would neigh, Atli, were you not gelded:
   Hrimgerd turns up her tail!
Your heart, I think, is behind your bottom,
   Though you roar like a randy stallion.''

"A stallion you will find me if you stay to prove me,
   Should I come ashore:
If so minded, I shall maul you well
   And twist your tail, Hrimgerd!''

"If you have the courage, come ashore!
  Let us meet in Varin's vik.
I shall break your ribs and rend you, warrior,
  Should you come within reach of my claws."

"I will not move till the men wake
  While I hold the hero's watch:
It would not surprise me if near our ship
  An ogress soon should surface."

"Awake, Helgi, and weregild pay
  For having slain Hati:
Let Hrimgerd bed with the boar for one night,
  And the recompense is paid."

"Lodin shall bed you, loathsome woman,
  The thurse who lives in Tholley:
Lodin, the worst of lava-field dwellers
  Is the meet mate for you."

"The woman you wish for watched over
  The harbour, Helgi, last night:
That gold-rich maiden has great power
  As showed when she came ashore
  To defend your fleet from danger.
Because of her I could not then
  Kill the king's host."

"Weregild you shall have, Hrimgerd, if you
  Will tell the talented prince:
Did one alone shield the ships of the king,
  Or did many guard them together?"

"Three nines there were, but one maiden
  Rode in front of the rest:
They rode mares from whose manes dropped
  Sweat into deep dales,
  Hail into high woods,
  Making the seasons for men.
  I hated every one."

"Look east, Hrimgerd: Helgi has now
   Struck you with Hel-staves:
On land and sea the leader's men
   And their ships are well shielded.

"It is dawn, Hrimgerd: Atli has delayed you,
   Your delay will last forever.
As a harbour-mark for men to laugh at
   You shall stand there like stone."

By now Helgi was an all-powerful warrior. He went to King Eylimi
to ask for the hand of his daughter, Svava. Helgi and Svava
exchanged vows and loved one another very much. Svava stayed at
home with her father while Helgi went to war.

At this time, Hjörvard's eldest son, Hedin, was living at home in
Norway. On Yule Eve he was riding home alone through the forest
when he met a troll-woman. She was riding a wolf and had snakes
for reins. She asked Hedin to go with her. "No," he said. "For
that," she said, "you shall pay at the bragging-toasts." That
evening binding vows were made; the sacred boar was brought in,
men laid their hands on it and swore oaths as they drank. Hedin
swore an oath to Svava, his brother Helgi's betrothed, but
immediately regretted it so much that he took to wild paths over the
land until he found his brother. Hrodmar's son, King Alf, had just
challenged Helgi to a duel at Sigarsvellir in three nights' time.
When Helgi saw his brother he said:

"What news, brother, do you bring from Norway?
Why have you left your land, Hedin,
And ridden wild roads to find me?"

"I bear a heavy burden of guilt,
For I chose your bride at the bragging-toasts."

"Do you blame yourself, brother; both of us know
That in ale-talk truth may be spoken.
I am challenged by Alf, Hrodmar's son
To a sword-meeting on Sigarsvellir
In three nights' time.
I cannot tell what will come of that,
Good luck or bad, but so be it."

"You have said, Helgi, that Hedin was worthy
Of great gifts, and of goods too.
It were better to bloody the sword
Than propose peace to foes."

Helgi said he believed that the wolf-rising woman Hedin had met
must have been his familiar spirit in disguise which meant that he
was now doomed to die. He said:

"She rode the wolf through the woods at night,
The woman asked Hedin to follow her:
She knew in her heart that Helgi must die,
Sigrlin's son, on Sigarsvellir."

There was a great battle in which Helgi was mortally wounded.

Helgi sent Sigar to find
Svava, Eylimi's only daughter,
And bid her be ready to ride quickly
If she hoped to find her hero alive.

"Helgi has sent me, Svava, to say this:
The one desire of the wounded warrior
Is to look on your face before he dies."

"A hard fate has befallen me.
What happened to Helgi, Hjörvard's son?
If the sea has drowned him or a sword bitten him,
I will avenge him, do harm to his foes."

"At Frekastein fell this morning
The best king under the bright sun.
Now Alf will rule over all."

"Hail, Svava! Let your heart be steady
At this, our last meeting on Middle-Earth.
From fatal wounds the warrior bleeds,
The sword-point came close to my heart.

"Svava, my bride, I beg you, weep not,
But listen well to my last request.
Prepare the bed for my brother, Hedin,
And lead to love the living boar."

"When we met, beloved, at Munaheim,
And you gave me a pledge-ring, I promised then
That I would never after your death
Take in my arms an untested warrior."

"Kiss me, Svava! You will not see me again,
Nor I Rogheim or Rödulsfell,
Till I have avenged the valiant son
Of a brave Hjörvard, the best of kings."

The Second Lay of Helgi, Hunding's Killer

King Sigmund, Völsung's son, married Borghild of Bralund. They named their son Helgi, after Helgi Hjörvardsson, and had Hagal foster him. Hunding was the name of a powerful king after whom Hundland is named. He was a great warrior and had many sons who went to work with him. Between Hunding and Sigmund was no peace, but great enmity. They slew one another's friends. King Sigmund and his clan were known as Völsungs and Ylfings. Helgi went and spied secretly among Hunding's men. Haeming, Hunding's son, was at home. When Helgi went there he met a herdsman, and asked him:

> "Say to Haeming that Helgi remembers
> Whom it was the warriors felled;
> The guest in your hall is a grey wolf,
> Thought to be Hamal by Hunding the king."

Hagal's son was called Hamal. Hunding sent his men to Hagal to look for Helgi, and Helgi could see no other way but to put on clothes of a bondsmaid and work at the mill. The men searched but did not find Helgi.

> Then said Blind, the bale-wise:
> "Keen are the eyes of Hagal's slave-maid;
> Of no churl's stock she who stands at the querns;
> The stones fracture, the flour-bin shakes.
>
> "A bitter fate has befallen the hero,
> That a leader must grind the grain of strangers;
> Better to his hand the haft of a sword
> Than the menial wood of a mill-handle."

Hagal answered and said:

> "Small harm is befallen, the flour-bin rattles,
> When the mill is turned by the maid of the king;
> She strode through the heavens, the uppermost skies
> And dared to fight as vikings are wont,
> Until Helgi took her captive.
> She is the sister of Sigar and Högni;
> Fierce-eyed is the Ylfings' daughter."

Helgi came from there and boarded a fighting vessel. He killed
Hunding and was from that time onward called Helgi Hunding's
Killer. He lay with his army in Brunavag where he wrought
slaughter on the beach and gnawed raw flesh. There was a king
called Högni whose daughter Sigrun was a valkyrie who rode the
wind and the waves. She was Svava reborn. Sigrun rode to the
ships and said:

> "Whose are the ships anchored in the firth?
> Where are your homes, heroes of war?
> For what do you bide in Brunavag?
> Which way do you wish to take?"

Hagal answered and said:

> "Hamal's are the ships, anchored in the firth.
> We have our homes in Hlesey.
> We bide for a breeze in Brunavag.
> Eastward the way we wish to take."

> "Where, chieftain have you waged battle,
> Or fed the geese of Gunnar's sister?
> Why is your byrnie blood-bespattered,
> Why under your helmet do you eat raw meat?"

> "A son of the Ylfings, I have returned
> From the western sea, if you want to know,
> Where I hunted the bear in Bragi's wood
> And with sword-point sated eagles.

> "Now, maiden, you know why it is
> That under my helmet I eat raw meat."

> "You proclaim victory. King Hunding
> Was felled to the earth by Helgi's sword.
> You advanced to the fight and avenged kinsmen;
> Blood gushed out when your blades struck."

> "Wise woman, whence do you know
> We are those who have vowed to avenge kinsmen?
> Many are brave who are born to warriors,
> Many who look much like our own."

"I was not far off; near I stood
Yesterday morning when the mighty one fell;
Sigmund's son is sly and devious
When in corpse-runes he tells his tale of battle.

Earlier I looked on the long ships,
When the folk-leader stood in the foremost prow,
And cold-wet waves washed about him.
Now Dag's kin deems he can deceive me,
But Helgi is known to Högni's maid.''

There was a powerful king called Granmar who lived at Svarins-mound. He had many sons; Hödbrod was one, Gudmund another, and Starkad a third. At the king's council Hödbrod was promised Sigrun, Högni's daughter. When she heard this, she rode the air and waterways with valkyries to find Helgi. Helgi was meanwhile in Logafell where he had fought against the sons of Hunding. He killed there Alf and Eyjolf, Hjörvard and Hervard, and, weary with battle, sat under Eaglestone. Sigrun found him there and threw herself about his neck, kissed him, and told him the news.

Sigrun greeted the glad king,
Took Helgi's hand: with him she would live.
She came to the king and kissed him then:
The hero's heart answered her wish.

Högni's daughter from her heart spoke,
Told Helgi she would have his love.
With Sigurd's son, she said boldly
She had fallen in love before she saw him.

I was promised to Hödbrod, with the host as witness
But another warrior I wished to have.
I fear prince, that my friends will be angry;
I have broken my father's fondest wish.''

Högni's daughter from her heart spoke,
Told Helgi she would have his love.

"Have no fear of Högni's wrath,
Nor of the anger of all your kin.
Young maiden, with me you shall live:
I fear not what your family may do.''

Helgi gathered together a great army of ships and travelled to
Wolfstone, but on the sea encountered a deadly storm. Lightning
flashed overhead and bolts struck the ship. They saw nine valkyries
riding the air and recognized Sigrun among them. Then the storm
calmed and they came safely to shore. Granmar's sons sat on a hill
as the ships sailed to land. Gudmund leapt on his horse and rode to
a hill near the harbour to spy. Gudmund, Granmar's son, asked:

> "Who commands this mighty fleet
> And a fierce host ferries ashore?
> Who is the Shielding whom the ships follow,
> Unfurling his banner before the mast?
> They seek no peace, it seems; the dawn
> Is battle-red about the vikings."

Sinfjötli said:

> "Here, Hödbrod, Helgi stands
> In the midst of his fleet: flee he will not;
> He rules your race, he rules Fjörsung's
> Inheritance, weighted under itself."

> "First we shall fight at Frekastein,
> Dispute the truth with our spear points:
> We have vowed, Hödbrod, to avenge our wrongs;
> Too long have we borne a baser share."

> "You shall tend goats, Gudmund, first,
> And climb the rifts of rocky fells;
> You hold in your hand a hazel-club,
> More friendly to you than the fate of the waves."

> "It would better beseem you, Sinfjötli,
> To fight a battle and fatten eagles
> Than to do nothing, duelling with words,
> While the ring-breakers wage their feuds.

> "Granmar's sons mean no good, I think,
> But to say the truth beseems a king;
> They manifested on Moinsheim
> Doughty hearts when they drew their swords;
> Bold and brave are these boar-warriors."

Gudmund rode home with tidings of the battle, while Granmar's
sons gathered an army. Many kings assembled. There was Högni,
Sigrun's father, and his sons Bragi and Dag. There was a great
battle of Granmar's sons and thanes were killed except Dag who
swore oaths to the Völsungs. Sigrun went among the corpses and
found Hödbrod dying. She said:

> "Never shall Sigrun of Sefafell
> Sink in the arms of Hödbrod the king.
> The host is scattered — often the troll-wolf
> Gripped the wrists of Granmar's sons."

Then she came upon Helgi and was overjoyed. He said:

> "Not all was good that was given you,
> Though the Norns, too, are not blameless:
> There fell this morning at Frekastein
> Bragi and Högni; I was their killer;

> "At Styrkleifar Starkad the king,
> And at Hlebjörg Hrollaug's sons.
> There I saw the most savage of beasts,

> "For the trunk fought on when the head was severed.
> Many corpses of your kindred lie
> Lifeless on the ground, a great host.
> You have not won victory; the Norns decreed
> That you should bring mighty men to their deaths.

> "But take heart, Sigrun, you were Hild to me:
> Shieldings are powerless to oppose their fate."
> "Could I have my wish, the host would be alive:
> Let me bury myself in your bosom now."

Helgi married Sigrun and they had sons. Helgi did not live to old
age. Dag, Högni's son, sacrificed to Odin to avenge his father, and
Odin presented Dag with his spear. Dag found his brother-in-law
at Fetter-wood, and thrust him through with the spear. Helgi fell
dead and Dag rode to the mountains to tell Sigrun the news.

"Alas, sister, I have sorrowful news,
For my kin grieve against my will:
This morning there fell under Fjötur's wood
The mightiest prince on Middle-Earth,
He who stood high upon heroes' necks."

"Your broken oaths shall bite your flesh,
All your vows to Helgi sworn
Beside the bright seas of Leiptur,
At the Rock-of-Waves, wet with spray.

"May the ship not sweep out when on you would sweep,
Though a wished-for breeze blow behind it,
May the horse not run though run you bid it,
When you would flee from your foes in battle.

"May the sword not bite when you brandish it
Unless on your own head it should sing.
I would treat you, Helgi's killer,
Like a wild wolf in the woods alone,
Without goods, without pleasures,
Stuffing on corpses lest you starve else."

Dag said:

"You are out of your senses, sister, raving,
To wish such ill to your own brother.
Odin alone wields all curses,
Who stirs up kinsmen with strife-runes.

"Your brother offers you bright rings,
All Vandilsve and Vigdal;
Take half the world as weregild,
Ring-adorned Sigrun, for your sons and you.

"Grieving I sit at Sefafell,
I shall never rejoice, not in my lifetime,
Unless the hero's light burst forth,
And Vigblaer, guided by the gold bit,
Bear him hither: I would be happy then.

"As, full of fear, the fell goats
Frantically run from the fierce wolf,
So did Helgi sow terror
In the hearts of his foes and all their kin.

"As an ash-tree rises over the thorn,
Or the young fawn, flecked with dew,
Climbs high above all the beasts,
His horns glowing up to heaven itself,
So was Helgi higher than all other warriors."

A cairn was raised to Helgi's memory, and when he arrived in Valhalla, Odin had him rule with him. Helgi said:

"You, Hunding, shall be slave to every man,
Wash their feet and their fire kindle,
Tie up the dogs and tend the horses,
Give swill to the swine and not sleep till then."

Sigrun's handmaiden went one evening to Helgi's cairn and saw Helgi riding to the grave with many men. She said:

"What mean these phantoms I fancy I see?
The doom of the gods? Dead men ride,
Pricking their horses with the points of their spurs.
Are home journeys granted to heroes when dead?

"We are no phantoms that you fancy you see;
Time has not ended though on us you look,
Pricking our horses with the points of our spurs:
Home journeys are not granted to heroes when dead."

She went home and said to Sigrun:

"Go forth, Sigrun, from Sefafell
If you wish to find the folk-leader.
The grave is open, Helgi has come,
 Helgi the king: the kin of Dag
Asks you to bind his bleeding wounds."

Sigrun went into Helgi's grave and said:

> "I am as merry at our meeting now.
> As the wolfish hawks of Odin the wise
> When they witness the slaughter of warm flesh
> Or behold the dawn dew-besprinkled.

> "I will kiss the unliving king although
> Your bloody byrnie is unbuckled still;
> Your hair, Helgi, is hoar-frosted,
> My prince is all speckled with slaughter-dew,
> Cold are the hands of Högni's kin;
> How, my prince, can I heal your wounds?"

> "Sigrun from Sefafell, you decided my fate,
> The sprinkling of Helgi with harm's dew.
> Blood drips from the breast of your king
> You shall shed tender tears for me,
> Gold-cold, grief-stifled,
> Before you sleep, sun-bright maiden.

> "Well shall we drink a draught together
> Though love and lands are lost to us.
> Let no man sing a song of grief
> Though bloody wounds in my breast may be seen.
> Now shining brides are shut in graves,
> Daughters of men, with the dead host."

Sigrun prepared a bed in the grave

> "Here my prince, I have prepared a bed;
> I shall not sorrow for the son of Ylfings,
> But sleep I will, as once I did
> With my living love, on my leader's breast."

> "Never till now have I known such a marvel,
> Soon or late in Sefafell.
> Behold Sigrun, Högni's daughter,
> Born of kings, as a bride sleeping
> In unliving arms while living still!

"It is time for me to ride the red ways,
Tread with my horse the heaven's road
Away to the west of Windhelm's bridge,
Before Salgofnir wakes the warriors to battle."

Helgi rode off on his way and the women returned to their dwelling.
The next evening Sigrun had her handmaid watch over the cairn,
and at sunset Sigrun herself came to the grave. She said:

"If minded to come, he would have come by now,
Helgi the hero, from Odin's dwelling;
Grey have my hopes grown with waiting,
For eagles sit on the ash-boughs:
To the Thing-of-Dreams they drive all lords."

"Be not so mad, maid of the Shieldings,
As to enter alone the House of the Dead:
Dead friends are more fell by night,
In the dark hours, than when dawn has broken."

Sigrun's life was shortened by grief and sorrow. It was believed in
the old days that men were reborn, but that is now called an old
wives' tale. Yet, it was said that Helgi and Sigrun were reborn, he
as Helgi Hadding's killer and she as Kara, Halfdan's daughter,
just as it is said in the lay of Kara that she was a valkyrie.

The Lay of Hlöd

(The Battle of the Huns and the Goths)

Of old by Humli the Huns were ruled,
The Gauts by Gizur, the Goths by Angantyr,
The Danes by Valdar, the Gauls by Kjar,
And Alrek the Wolf ruled the English nation.

In Hunland then, in the holy wood,
Heidrek's son, Hlöd was raised,
With byrnie and sword, with sax and helmet,
ring-adorned, and a racing mare.

He rode from the East to ask for his portion,
To Arheim he came, to the court of the Goths;
Angantyr there with his thanes was sitting
At a funeral feast for their father Heidrek.

Before the gates he found a warrior;
Weary with travel, these words he spoke:
"Go to Angantyr in his great hall
And ask him now to answer me."

Warrior   "Hither has come Heidrek's son,
The battle-brewer, your brother Hlöd;
Mighty he looks on is mare's back;
He wishes, king, for a word with you."

In the hall an uproar arose;
All wished to hear what Hlöd would say,
And what answer Angantyr would give his brother.

Angantyr   "Hail to you, Hlöd, Heidrek's son!
Let us sit, my brother, on the bench together,
And drink from beakers of beer or wine
To Heidrek our father, the first of men."

Hlöd   "I will have half of what Heidrek left,
Cows and calves and corn-mills,
Awls and arrows, useful treasure,
Thralls and bondmaids and their children.

"That famed heath, the forest Mirkwood,
The sacred grave beside the Dneipr,
Half the armour that Heidrek possessed,
Land and people and polished rings."

Angantyr   "First, brother, bone-white lances
And cold spears will clash and break,
And many lie without life in the grass,
Before I halve my heritage with you,
Or divide Tyrfing into two parts.

"I will gladly give you gleaming spears,
Fulfil your wish with wealth and treasure,
Twelve hundred men, twelve hundred mares,
And twelve hundred armed serfs,

"To each of your men much to accept,
Nobler gifts than he now has,
To each man a maid to accept,
And on each maid I will hang a necklace.

"Your weight in silver as you sit there
I will give you and throw down gold as you leave,
So that rings shall roll around your path;
A third of the Goths you shall govern alone."

At that time Gizur Grytingalidi, King Heidrek's foster-father, was staying with King Angantyr. He was very old. When he heard Angantyr's offer, he thought it was over-generous and said:

Gizur   "This is a bargain for a bondmaid's child,
A bondmaid's child though born of a king:
When the valiant lords were dividing the heritage,
The bastard sat by himself on a howe."

King Humli asked what had been talked about. When he heard that Hlöd, his daughter's son, had been called the son of a bond-maid, he grew very angry and said:

Humli   "We will pass the winter in peace at home,
          Biding our time while we talk and drink,
          Teaching the Huns to train for battle,
          Till ready as wolves for war-play.

          "We will give you a host, Hlöd, my grandson,
          Of warriors ready to wage battle,
          With many twelve-winter and two-winter horses,
          Muster the army of Huns for war."

At sunrise one morning, as Hervor stood on the keep over the fortress and looked southward towards the forest, she saw a great cloud of dust rising, so huge that it hid the sun for a long time. She realized that it was the Huns approaching and in great numbers. She said to Ormar: "Ride to meet the Huns and offer them battle before the south gate of the fortress." Ormar said:

Ormar   "I will willingly ride and wield a sword,
          Go to war for the Gothic people."

Hervor fell and a great host about her. When Ormar saw her fall, he rode day and night until he stood before Angantyr.

Ormar   "I have come from the south with cruel tidings:
          Burned with fire is the forest of Mirkwood,
          Bathed in gore is the Gothic host.

          "Heidrek's daughter, Hervor, your sister,
          Has fallen in battle, felled by the Huns,
          And many thousands of your thanes also.

          "She was lighter in battle than in lover's words,
          Or in walking to the bench in a wedding procession."

Angantyr   "When we drank mead there were many of us,
          Now there are few when we need more.

"In my troop what man is left
Who, though I gave him gleaming rings,
Would willingly ride and wield a sword,
Call the hosts of the Huns to battle?"

Gizur "I will not ask for an ounce of gold,
That clinking demon which brings doom to men,
But will willingly ride and wield a sword,
Call the hosts of the Huns to battle:
Where shall we brave them with battle-staves?"

Angantyr "Dare them to fight on Dunheath,
To join in battle under Jassarfell:
There Goths have often gone to war,
Won fame and fair victory."

Gizur rode away until he came to the army of the Huns.

Gizur "Dread is upon you, doomed is your leader,
For Odin is angry: hoist your banners.

"I dare you go fight on Dunheath,
To join in battle under Jassarfell.
Let Odin fly the arrow as I say."

Hlöd "Seize Gizur Grytingalidi,
Gizur from Arheim, Angantyr's man."

But Gizur rode back to King Angantyr.

Gizur "In six units are the warrior folk,
And each folk is five thousand,
In each thousand thirteen hundred,
In each hundred heroes four times counted."

On the next day they joined battle and fought all day long.
Angantyr went to search the field for the slain and found his brother
Hlöd. Then he said:

Angantyr   "I would have given you gleaming spears,
Fulfilled your wish with wealth and treasure:
Now, neither with rings nor with lands
But with battle, brother, have you been paid.

"I was fated to kill you: a curse was on us,
As the Norns decreed: It shall never be forgotten."

The Waking of Angantyr

A young maiden met at sunset
A man with his flock on Munarvag.

Herdsman   "To visit this island all alone
Is overbold: go back to your lodging."

Hervör   "I have no lodging: of the island folk
I know none. I will not go back.
Before we part, first tell me
How I may come to the Hjörvard graves."

Herdsman   "Do not ask: it is unwise.
You do not know your deadly peril:
Let us flee as fast as our feet can take us,
All without is a horror to view."

Hervör   "It is vain to hinder the viking's friend.
Show me the way: as a reward you shall have
This gold necklace: you will get nothing,
Nor ring nor ornament if you hold your peace."

Herdsman   "To have come hither, all alone
To this land of shadows, was sheer folly.
Over fen and fold fires are soaring,
Graves are opening: let us go quickly."

Hervör   "Fear not the fire, fear not the graves:
Although the island be all aflame,
Never shall warriors while they live
Yield to terror. Tell me the way."

The herdsman had taken to his heels already,
Fled to the wood, far from the maiden,
But the fierce heart in Hervör's breast
Swelled up at the sight of these things."

She saw now the grave-fires and the graves standing open. She
went to the howe and was not afraid. She passed the fires as if they
were smoke, until she reached the graves of the berserks. Then she
said:

Hervör   "Angantyr, wake! Hervör calls you,
       Your only daughter whom you had by Tofa.
       Give up from the grave the gleaming sword
       That the dwarves smithied for Svafrlami.

       "Hervard, Hjörvard, Hrani, awake!
       Hear me, all of you, under the tree-roots,
       With sharp swords, with shields and byrnies
       And red spears, the rig of war.

       "Much are you changed, children of Arngrim,
       Once so mighty: are you mold now?
       Will Eyfura's sons refuse to listen
       Or speak with me on Munarvag?

       "May ants shred you all to pieces,
       Dogs rend you; may you rot away.
       Give back the sword that was smithied by Dvalin:
       Fine weapons are unfit for ghosts."

Angantyr   "Evil it is, Hervör, my daughter,
       To call down such curses upon us:
       Your words are mad, without meaning in them.
       Why do you wake the bewildered dead?

       "Nor father nor brothers buried me deep.
       Tyrfing was owned by two who live,
       Though only one owned it later."

Hervör   "Tell me the truth, that the timeless gods
       May bless your grave. Have you got Tyrfing?
       Why are you unwilling to yield
       Your heritage to your only child?"

Then it was as if a flame lit up all the graves which stood open. Then Angantyr said:

Angantyr   "Graves open and Hel's doors,
           The island surface is one searing flame,
           All without is a horror to view:
           Go, while there's time: return to your ship."

Hervör   "With no flames, tonight or ever,
           With no fire can you frighten me,
           Nor daunt the heart in your daughter's breast
           With ghosts standing at grave-mouths."

Angantyr   "Hear me, Hervör, hear from me now,
           Daughter of princes, the doom I foretell:
           This Tyrfing will, if the true blade,
           Destroy your kindred, kill them all.

           "You will bear a son, a bold warrior,
           Who shall wield Tyrfing, trust in its strength:
           After Heidrek shall the hero be named,
           The bravest one under heaven's tent."

Hervör   "Churlish cowards! May my curse fall
           On all of you: may you ever lie,
           Wretched shades, in the rot of the pit.
           Give back the wondrous work of smiths:
           Son of vikings, it is vain to hide it."

Angantyr   "No mortal maiden to me you seem,
           Who walk in the dark where the dead lie,
           Uncowed by flames, with a carved spear
           And mailed corselet on Munarvag."

Hervör   "A mortal maiden to men I seemed
           Until advised to visit your halls:
           Surrender the blade, the bane-of-shields,
           Hater-of-byrnies, Hjalmar's-killer."

Angantyr   "Hjalmar's-killer lies under my shoulders,
The sharp sword, sheathed in flame:
No maiden on earth, no mortal dare
Touch such a weapon, take it to hold."

Hervör   "I will touch the weapon, take hold of
The sharp edge. In order to get it
I will walk through fire with unflinching step:
The flames are sinking before my eyes."

Angantyr   "Reckless maiden, rather than see you
Fling yourself on the flames and perish,
I will grant what you ask, give you the blade:
Such courage of heart I cannot refuse."

Hervör   "You have done well, dead warrior,
To grant what I ask, give me the blade:
To possess the sword seems to me better
Than to own all Norway."

Angantyr   "Alas, daughter, little you know,
Wretched woman, at what you rejoice
I tell you again, this Tyrfing will
Destroy your kindred, kill them all."

Hervör   "With a glad heart I will go now
To ride the horses of the roaring sea:
Little care I what may come after,
What dole my sons may deal each other."

Angantyr   "Long may you hold it and long enjoy it!
But conceal it well. Beware the edges
Of Hjalmar's-Bane: both are poisoned.
Mortal to man is the Measurer-of-Fate.

"Farewell, daughter: would I could give you
All the strength and stoutness of heart
That was taken from Arngrim's twelve sons,
The good of life they lost in death."

Hervör "I will hasten hence: I am eager to be gone.
Blessed in your graves, may you be at peace.
I deemed in my mind that death was near
When all about me leaped high flame."

The Treachery of Asmund

Innstein "Let us go landgates, leaving the ships,
All our host, all the spearmen,
To burn Asmund's hall with fire,
Fall on his troops and take their lives."

Half "We should send, rather, a small band
To march from the sea and make peace:
Asmund has offered in earnest of friendship
Many rings of red gold."

Innstein "Small insight have you into Asmund's mind;
The king is cunning, cruel in heart:
I counsel you, prince, to put little
Store of trust in your step-father."

Half "Asmund has pledged his promise to us
With solemn oaths as are sworn among men:
A good king will not go against his word,
Will never betray another warrior."

Innstein "Odin, Half, must be angry with you:
Unwise your faith in the word of the king.
Asmund, I tell you, will betray us unless
We guard ourselves against his wiles."

Half "It pleases you well to prophesy ill.
The king will surely keep the peace:
Good-will and welcome await us in his court,
Rings of gold and rich jewels."

Innstein "A dream came to me — dwell on it, Half!
Fierce flames flickered about us;
To break loose was no light work.
What meaning, prince, do you make of my dream?"

Half   "That I shall give a gleaming helmet
To each bold fighter who follows me;
Helmets will blaze like bright fire
On the hair-hills of the host of Skjöldungs."

Innstein   "My second dream — consider it, Half!
My shoulders were scorched, shrivelled by flames;
Ill, not good, my heart forebodes.
What meaning, prince, do you make of my dream?"

Half   "That bright on the backs of battle-wise warriors,
Shining on the shoulders of the shield-bearers,
Of each bold fighter who follows me,
Golden byrnies shall blaze like fire."

Innstein   "My third dream — think on it, Half!
We all lay dead in the depths of the sea,
Betrayed by the wiles of the troll-like chief.
What meaning, prince, do you make of my dream?"

Half   "Enough! I have listened too long to your fears.
I command you, Innstein, to hold your peace
And speak no more in my hearing
From henceforth of your foolish dreams."

Innstein   "Hearken to me, men of Rogaland,
Hearken, Hrok, and Utstein too;
Let the host now landgates march,
Nor trust, like Half, in Asmund's word."

Utstein   "Let us, rather, allow our prince
To say what shall be, decide our journey:
Let us follow him; if our fearless leader
So rule, we will risk our lives."

Innstein   "Of old my prince took pleasure in my counsel
Many times we marched forward,
But since we landed on this luckless shore,
My words are not spoken to a will to hear."

They went to Asmund's Hall, feasted and fell asleep. When they woke, the hall was filled with smoke. They armed themselves and prepared for battle. Innstein said:

> "There is smoke above the hawks in the Hall of the
> king;
> Wax from our sword-points soon will drip.
> It is time for the gold, the twinkling gems,
> And the helmets to be offered to Half's warriors.
>
> "Awake, Half! All about us
> Your grim-minded kin have kindled fires;
> Jewels of flame are the gems they offer,
> Pleasing presents you must pay back.
>
> "Finish, friends, the foaming ale,
> The stout pillars are starting to crack.
> Men shall remember while men live
> The march of our host to the maker-of-war.
>
> "Go boldly forward nor fall back:
> Our foes shall learn to fear our sword-play;
> Cruel scars they shall carry hence,
> Bloody limbs before the battle ends.
>
> "Brave youths, break through the wall
> Of glowing fire with our gallant prince;
> No man is allowed to live forever:
> The furnisher of rings will not flinch at death."

They broke out of the hall, but Half fell among his men. Innstein said:

> "I have watched them all, as one following,
> Equal in courage, the king's son;
> We shall meet again when we go hence;
> Life is a burden no lighter than death.

"Hrok has fallen at the feet of his prince,
The young warrior, wolf-bold:
It is ill to yield up to All-Father,
Robbed of victory, so valiant a man.

"For eighteen summers I have set forth ,
Ridden with the host to redden our spears:
Never shall I know another lord
Nor gladness in battle, nor grow old.

"Stretched on the earth shall Innstein lie,
Here by the head of Half, his prince:
Men shall remember while men live
That the Lord of Rogaland laughed as he died."

The Lay of Hyndla

Freya   "Wake, noble maiden, wake, dear friend,
In your cavern home; Hyndla, wake!
The Great Twilight is come; we two shall ride
To Valhalla, to the holy place.

"Let us ask Host-Father for his favour now:
Red gold he gives the deserving,
To Hermod he gave a helmet and byrnie,
To Sigmund a sword to wield.

"To some he gives victory, to some riches,
Eloquence to many, to men understanding,
Fair winds to the valiant, verse to skalds,
And might he grants to many warriors.

"To Thor, the Hammerer, I will offer sacrifice,
That he in your need may never forsake you,
Though he has little love for trolls.

"Fetch one of your wolves from their wooden stall,
And let him run a race with my boar."

Hyndla   "Your boar will not run on the roads to the gods;
I will not saddle my swart mare.

"You are deceitful, so to test me,
Fixing me, Freya, with your fierce eyes:
Ottar the young, Innstein's son,
Your favourite, keeps the company of the dead."

Freya   "You are dense, Hyndla, you dream when you say
That Ottar the young, Innstein's son,
My favourite, keeps the company of the dead.
See where my boar glows, the battle-swine,
In his gold-bristled skin, skilfully fashioned
By two dwarves, Dain and Nabbi.

"Now let the two of us talk from our saddles,
And reckon up the races of kings,
Name all their kin who came from the gods.

"Ottar the young and Angantyr
Have made wagers in the metal of Gaul:
It is my duty to help the young man,
That he may live to inherit his realm.

"He piled up boulders to build me an altar;
Those rocks are turned already to glass;
He has reddened that cairn with cattle-blood:
In goddesses Ottar always had faith.

"You shall relate now the lineages of men,
Tell from what ancestors each is descended,
Who from the Skilfings and the Skjöldungs,
Who from the Öldings, who from the Ylfings,
Who are high-born, who are free-born,
Most chosen of mortals on Middle-Earth."

Hyndla   "You, Ottar, by Innstein were begotten
As to Alf the old Innstein was,
Alf by Ulf, Ulf by Saefari,
And Saefari by Svan the red.

"Your father's mother had many a necklace,
Her name, if you ask me, was Hledis the priestess:
Frodi was her father, Frjaut her mother;
More than mortal men deemed them.

"Ali was stronger in earlier days,
Before him Halfdan, highest of the Skjöldungs;
Famed were the folk-wars that fighter waged,
The rumours of his deeds rose to the heavens.

"With a sword he slew Sigtrygg and vowed
Blood-brotherhood with Eymund, boldest of men;
He married Almveig, great-hearted woman;
Together they had eighteen sons.

"Thence come the Skjöldungs, thence the Skilfings,
Thence the Ödlings, thence the Ynglings,
Thence the high-born, thence the free-born,
Most chosen of mortals on Middle-Earth.
All these were your ancestors, Ottar the foolish.

"Almveig's mother was Hildigun,
The child of Svava the sea-king.
All these were your ancestors, Ottar the foolish.
Remember them all. What more would you know?

"Dag wed Thora; to them were born heroes,
Bold fighters, a family of warriors,
Both the Frekis, Frodmar and Gyrd,
Alf the old, Arm and Jösurmar:
All these were your ancestors, Ottar the foolish.

"Ketil was their kinsman, Klypp's heir;
It was he who begot your grandmother;
Then there was Frodi before Kari,
And earlier still was Alf begotten.

"Nanna came next, Nökkvi's daughter,
Your father's daughter affianced her son:
Old is this friendship; further I tell
That I knew Hörvi and Brod.
All these were your ancestors, Ottar the foolish.

"I will relate your lineage further,
Tell of Isolf and Asolf, Ölmod's sons,
And of Skurhild, Skekkil's daughter:
All these were your ancestors, Ottar the foolish.

"Gunnar the bulwark, Grim the ploughshare,
Yawning Ulf and Ironshield Thorir,

"Bui and Brami, Barri and Reifnir,
Tind and Tyrfing and the two Haddings:
All these were your ancestors, Ottar the foolish.

"Ani and Omi were also born
To Arngrim and Eyfura,
Boisterous berserks of baleful deeds;
Over fell and firth like fire they sped:
All these were your ancestors, Ottar the foolish.

"I knew them both, Brod and Hörvi:
Hrolf the Old led the host they marched in;
By Jörmunrek these men were begotten.
Kin of Sigurd, pay count to my tale
Of how Fafnir was bested by that fierce king.

"The valiant leader was of Völsung stock;
Hjördis sprang from Hraudung,
Eylimi from the Ödlings:
All these were your ancestors, Ottar the foolish.

"Then there was Gudrun, Gjuki's daughter,
And Gunnar and Högni, Gjuki's sons;
Guthorm was not of Gjuki stock,
Although he was brother to both of them:
All these were your ancestors, Ottar the foolish.

"Harold Battle-Tooth was born to Hrörek,
The ring-slinger, and rich Auda;
Auda herself was Ivar's daughter,
And Radbard was Randver's father.

*   *   *

"Legend relates that eleven gods
Were there when Baldur the beautiful fell:
Vali vowed to avenge his death,
With his bow he slew his brother's killer.

"Baldur's father was Bur's heir,
Frey wed Gerd, Gymir's daughter
And Aurboda's both bred from the giants;
Thjazi the Mighty-Thewed was their kinsman,
The gale-eager giant who begot Skadi.

"Much have I told you, and more I will:
Remember it well. What more would you know?

"Hak was the best of all Hvaedna's sons,
Hvaedna was Hjörvard's father,
Heid and Hrossthjof were Hrimnir's kin.

"All sybils devolve from Vidolf,
All warlocks devolve from Vilmeid,
All sorcerers from Svarthöfdi,
From Ymir are descended all the giants.

"Much have I told you, and more I will.
Remember it well. What more would you know?

"There was one who lived long ago,
Of great strength, the gods' kinsman:
Nine giant maidens their mother bore
At the earth's edge to this honoured man.

"He begot Gjalp and Greip also,
He begot Eistla and Eyrgjafa,
He begot Ulfrun and Angeyja,
Imd and Atla and Jarnsaxa;

"Much I have told you, and more I will.
Remember it well. What more would you know?

"With boar's blood he bettered his strength,
With the might of the earth and the ice-cold sea.

"Much have I told you, and more I will.
Remember it well. What more would you know?

"Angrbod bore Fenris, fathered by Loki,
Who begot Sleipnir on Svadilfari:
But one monster was the worst of all;
From Byleist's brother that beast came.

"Loki found on a fire of lime-wood
A woman's heart which he ate half-cooked;
Lopt became pregnant by the poison in it;
All female monsters are the fruit of that.

"The sea rises to the ramparts of heaven,
The sky cracks open, the earth is drowned;
Soon will come snow and savage gales;
The fall of the gods is not far off.

"One was begotten, greater than all.
His might increased by the might of the earth;
The richest king he is called among men,
Sib of siblings in the sword-host.

"One more will come, mightier still,
A doughtier one I dare not name;
Further now can few see,
But Odin remembered to meet the wolf."

*　　*　　*

Freya　"Bear to my boar the beer of memory,
That he may have power to repeat the words
Uttered in the morning three morrows hence,
When Angantyr tells the tale of his kin."

Hyndla　"Leap into the night. I long to sleep.
Nothing good shall you get from me.
Friend of snakes, flee into darkness,
As Heidrun runs with the he-goats.

"Ever lustful, to Öd you ran;
Many hastened under your skirts.
Friend of snakes, flee into darkness,
As Heidrun runs with the he-goats."

Freya　"With red flames I surround you, giantess;
You cannot leave your cavern now."

Hyndla   ''Fires I see rising, flames from the earth,
Many will soon suffer death.
Carry beer, blended with poison,
To Ottar's hand in an evil day.''

Freya   ''Your cruel curse shall come to nothing,
Your threat of bale, bride of a giant.
A precious ale shall the hero drink:
I bid all the gods show grace to Ottar.''

Hjalmar's Death-Song

Hjörvard challenged Hjalmar to a duel south on Samsey. After the two brothers came home they prepared themselves for the duel. Their father led them to the ship where he gave Angantyr his sword Tyrfing. Hjalmar and Odd had gone up on the island to see if the Berserks had arrived, and when they came down from the forest to their ships the Berserks rushed out of the ships with bloody weapons, swords drawn.

Odd   "I felt afraid when first they came
With loud cries from the long ships,
And landed, howling, on the island shore,
Twelve together without glory or fame."

Hjalmar   "They are bold fighters who fare from the warships,
Twelve together without glory or fame:
I foresee that with Odin we shall sleep to-night,
Two brothers, but the twelve will live."

Odd   "Thus I answer those words:
I foresee that with Odin they will sleep to-night,
Twelve berserks, but we two shall live.

"One shall fight one, war-eager,
Unless he be fearful or faint of heart."

In the fight between Hjalmar and Angantyr, Hjalmar received sixteen wounds, but Angantyr fell dead.

Odd   "How fare you, Hjalmar? Your face is changed,
Your helmet hewed, your armour split:
I lie not when I say your life is over."

Hjalmar   "My armour is split, I have sixteen wounds,
I cannot see, my sight is darkened,
My heart was pierced by Angantyr's sword,
The steel-edge, steeped in venom.

"The farms I possessed were five in all,
But no joy have I known from these,
Bereft of life, I must lie down,
Sword-wounded on Samsey's shore.

"Ale in the hall the housecarls drink,
Honoured with jewels in the hall of my father;
Many a man is mead-weary,
But a cruel sword-spoor keeps me here.

"I left the white lady of the cloak
On the outer shore of Agnafit;
It has turned out true what she told me then,
That I would never come home again.

"Take the red-ring from my right hand,
Bring it to Ingibjörg, the beautiful maiden;
A lasting sorrow it will seem to her
That Uppsala will see me no more.

"I left the sweet songs of women,
Hurried away, eastward with Soti,
Joined a troop and journeyed on
For the last time from my loving comrades.

"No woman on earth shall ever learn
That I flinched from strokes on the field of battle
Or gave way; she will not laugh,
That swift minded woman in Sigtuna.

"I left Ingibjörg, the lovely maiden
The fated day was fixed already;
A hard-grasping grief to her it will be
That never again shall we greet each other.

"Bring her, I beg you, the byrnie of Hjalmar
And show it her, Odd, in the hall of the king;
The heart will leap in the leader's child
When she sees the gashes, grim in his armour.

"I see them sitting in Sigtuna,
Who tried in vain to prevent my journey;
Nor ale nor warriors in the hall of the king
Shall ever again gladden Hjalmar.

"The swift raven swoops from the east
Out of the tree, the eagle with him:
With raw flesh I feed the eagle
For the last time; he shall taste my blood."

Then Hjalmar died. Angantyr and his brothers were buried together with their weapons in a mound on Samsey.

Hildebrand's Death-Song

When Hildebrand struck with his sword on the helmet of Asmund, it broke just below the hilt and the blade fell into the water. He was weary from his many wounds. He then said to his brother:

> "It is hard to bear that one brother should
> Be fated to become the killer of the other:
> God led you from the land of Denmark,
> Brought you to meet with me in Sweden.

> "Two swords there were, weapons for glory,
> Gifts from Budli: now broken is the second.
> Dead dwarves made them in days long ago;
> None such have been forged, before or after.

> "By my head now lies my broken shield;
> On it ten eights have been notched,
> The count of the warriors killed by me.

> "My beloved son lies there also,
> My only offspring; by my head he lies,
> Denied life: that was not wished for.

> "One boon, brother, I bid of you,
> One favour that few killers
> Would do for another, but do it for me:
> Wrap me in weeds you have worn yourself.

> "Deprived of life, I must lie here
> Wounded by the sword that brought woe to us both."

Then Hildebrand, the Hunnish warrior, died. Asmund gave him a fitting burial, and pondered on the evil of fratricide. He met with no one else, so rode on to the town where his mother lived with the king's daughter, Aess the Fair. Asmund decided to ask for her hand. As he came through the doors of the hall, he said:

"Little was I ready, little prepared
That I should be called before other men,
That I should be chosen as champion of the Huns,
To be challenged eight times for the chieftain's kingdom.

"I fought against one, I fought against two,
I fought with four, then with five warriors,
I fought with six, then with seven at once,
Then alone against eight though I live still.

"My heart trembled, I was troubled greatly
When eleven challenged my championship,
Until Disir told me in my sleep
To fear not but fight them all.

"Then Hildebrand came. He was old in years,
The Hunnish warrior, and weak he seemed:
On him, under his helm, I marked
Hard tokens of war, wounds of death."

Thereafter men called him Asmund, the killer of heroes.

The Lay of Erik

Odin   "Before dawn in a dream I saw
Valhalla preparing to honour the dead;
Busy at my bidding was the band of warriors,
Benches they strewed and beer-jugs washed,
And the valkyrie brought out the best wine.
I expect men from Middle-Earth,
Great warriors such as gladden my heart.

"Bragi, it thunders like a thousand fighters,
   A mighty host is on the march."

Bragi   "The benches tremble as though Baldur were coming
   Back to Odin's hall."

Odin   "Foolish are your words, wise Bragi,
   Erik it is, as you know,
For whom all echoes: he will enter soon,
   The boar, into Odin's Hall.

"Sigmund! Sinfjötli! swiftly now
   Go to greet the prince
And bid him welcome, if he be Erik,
   The hero I am expecting."

Sigmund   "Why Erik rather than other princes?"

Odin   "In many lands he has marched to battle
   And borne a bloody sword."

Bragi   "Why rob of victory so valiant a man?"

Odin   "Why knows what awaits us? Even now he peers,
   The Grey Wolf, into the Gods' dwelling."

Sigmund   "Hail, Erik! Valhalla greets you.
        You are welcome, wise one, here.
    Tell me, I ask, what troop follows you,
        Boars from the clash of blades?"

    Erik   "Famous are they all, five kings:
        I am the sixth myself."

The Song of the Grinders

Two tellers of the future, Fenja and Menja,
Have come now to the King's house,
Troll maidens, taken into bondage,
To work for Frodi, Fridleif's son .

They were led off to a hand-mill
And commanded to grind grain all day:
Frodi told them they should take no rest,
Until he heard the tune of the bondmaids.

As they churned the handle, they chanted their song:
"Let us leave the mill and lift stones."
"Grind on", he ordered the maidens.

They sang and slung the swinging stone
Till Frodi's household fell asleep:
Then at the mill Menja spoke.

Menja   "We grind for Frodi, grind him wealth,
Riches and happiness at the happy mill:
He sits by his treasure, he sleeps on feathers,
He wakes to joy. It is well ground.

"No man here shall hurt another,
Nor cause dole nor do murder.
None with a sword shall slay another,
Though his brother's killer lie bound at his feet."

But Frodi said: "Sleep not,
Or no longer than caged cuckoos in the hall,
Or as long as a tune takes to sing."

Menja   "Frodi, you were not full-wise,
Friend of men, when you made us bondmaids:
You regarded our strength and our good looks,
But you did not ask after our race.

"Hard was Hrungnir, hard was his father,
Thjazi was the strongest, though, of them all;
Idi and Aurnir, the hill-giant brothers
Were our blood-kin; we were born of them.

"Grinder had not left the grey fell,
Come out of the hard hall in the ground,
Nor hill-giant maids at the mill worked,
If we had not foreknown it all.

"For nine winters wild were our games,
Strengthened and nourished beneath the earth,
We maidens strove to do mighty deeds,
By ourselves we shifted solid rocks.

"We yanked rocks from the yard of the giant,
So that the ground began to shake,
We slung the heavy slab about,
The moving stone for men to take.

"Time passed: as prophetesses then,
We marched in Sweden among the folk,
We bit byrnies, we broke shields,
And moved unscathed through the mailed host.

"We deposed one king, we supported another,
To good Gothorm we gave help,
We were not at ease till Knui fell.

"So we acted for half a year,
And won fame among fighting men;
We reddened blades, we bit flesh
With sharp swords, we shed blood.

"But now we are come to the king's house,
Held in bondage without mercy;
Mud eats our feet, we freeze above
As we work the peace-mill; it is wearisome here.

"Let our hands stop and the stone with them,
I have ground as much as is my desire."

Fenja   Our hands shall not stop nor the stone with them
Till Frodi's fate is fully ground.

Our hands shall handle hard shafts,
Corpse-bloody weapons: awake, Frodi,
Awake, Frodi, if you wish to hear
Our old songs, our old tales.

I see fire burning before the burg in the east,
Signs of battle, a signal calls;
An armed host will be here soon,
Set fire to the dwelling before the king.

You will never hold Hleidur's throne
Nor red rings nor royal stones:
Grasp the quern handle even tighter,
We were not warmer in warrior's blood.

My father's girl ground mightily,
Already she saw many signs of death,
The huge beams burst from the stand,
But grind on, the iron holds fast.

Grind on! Yrsa's son
Will have her vengeance for Halfdan's death,
To Yrsa soon he will also be known
As son and brother; we both know that.''

With all their might the maidens ground,
The ungentle ones were in giant-mood:
The mill-shaft broke, the mill foundations
Crashed and the mill-stone was cracked in two.

The hill-giant bride then uttered these words:
''Frodi, we have ground your fate as we wished,
We women have labored long at the mill.''

Part II

The Niflung Poems

Gripir's Prophecy

Gripir was the name of Eylimi's son and Hjördis' brother. He ruled over many lands and was the wisest and most far-sighted of men. Riding alone, Sigurd came to Gripir's hall. He was easy to recognise. He met a man called Geitir outside the hall, and spoke with him. He asked:

"Who lives here in this dwelling? What is the name of this folk-king?"
"Gripir he is called, captain of men, who rules firmly over land and thanes."

"Is the wise king at home in his court? Will he deign to speak with me? Counsel is helpful for an untried man. I am eager to find Gripir."

"The happy king will ask me this: 'Who is the man who asks counsel of Gripir?'"
"I am called Sigurd; I am Sigmund's son. Hjördis is my mother."

Then Geitir went and spoke to Gripir: "Here outside stands a stranger; he is lordly in looks; he wishes to visit with you."

The lord of men went from his room and welcomed warmly the warrior guest: "You are welcome here; it is about time you have come. Geitir, attend to Grani."

They spoke much, and traded many words, wise men, warriors both. "Say to me," said Sigurd, "my mother's brother, if you know: What will become of my life?"

"You will be the greatest of all men under the sun, highest born of any boar-fierce prince, generous with gold and niggardly with cowardice, noble of mien and wise of word."

"Tell me, honest king, for more I ask, wise one, if you foresee what will first come in my life once I go from your court."

"First, chieftain, you will avenge your father, and have revenge, too, for Eylimi's suffering; you will kill the hardy and bold sons of Hunding. Victory is yours."

"Noble king, tell me, your kinsman, openly, since we speak from our hearts, do you see bold deeds for me, those which grasp highest fame under the vaulted sky?"

"Alone you shall battle the squamous serpent that greedy lies on Gnita-heath. You shall be the killer of both Regin and Fafnir. I speak the truth."

"Wealth enough I shall win if I better these men, as you openly say. Now think more and say further about what comes then in my life."

"You will find Fafnir's hoard, and take his treasure, load the gold on Grani's flanks, and then ride to Gjuki, the war-king."

"Bold king, speak more of this speech to me. Once there I am Gjuki's guest; but then what comes into my life?"

"On a high fell sleeps a king's daughter, bright in her byrnie. With the keen sword which slew Fafnir you will hew and cut the byrnie."

"The byrnie breaks, the girl speaks, she awakens from her sleep. What will the woman say to Sigurd that will be of good?"

"She will teach you, the mighty one, runes, all those charms men long to learn, everyone to utter, spells for healing. Hail, chieftain!"

"That is done, wisdom won, and I am ready to ride the broadways. Now think more and say further about what comes then in my life."

"You will arrive at Heimir's court, and be the folk-king's glad guest. It fades now, what I could see ahead. It's no use questioning me further."

"Now your words bring sorrow, since you cannot see further, chief. You know too much of grief for me, Gripir, to say it easily."

"Your life's youth lay before me, bright before my vision. But I can be wrong, not always right in counsel, nor prophecy. Gone is what I saw."

"I know of no one the world over, Gripir, who is more far-sighted than you. Be it loathsome or dishonorable or shame to my stature, do not hide the future."

"There is no blame awaiting you in life, assure yourself; for your name shall be highest among war-makers while the earth remains."

"Well, if it is done, it is a shame for me to leave you, king. Show me further what lies in my future, famed one, my mother's brother."

"I shall tell all to you, prince, since you force it; you shall find that I do not lie; your day of death is destined."

"I do not invite your wrath, folk-king, only your counsel, Gripir. I want to know surely, though it be ill, what I can expect before my hands."

"There is a woman at Heimir's, fair of skin, called Brunhild by men. She is the daughter of Budli, a worthy king, and Heimir fosters this hardminded maid."

"What is it to me if the maid be fair of skin, fostered by Heimir? I compel you, Gripir, say all of the fate you see before you."

"The fair of skin, the fosterchild of Heimir, will steal the greatest of pleasures from you; no sleep will you sleep, nor resolve fights, nor seek men's company, except you have that maid."

"What comfort awaits me? Say it, Gripir, if you see. Will I get to buy the maid with marriage gold, win the worthy king's daughter?"

"You two shall swear all manner of oaths full-fast, but neither will hold to them. One night Gjuki's guest, and you will forget the fair fosterchild of Heimir."

"How is that, Gripir? Explain. Is there fickleness in my form that I should break word with a woman that in my heart would love?"

"Prince, you are in the snares of another, and must suffer Grimhild's deceit. She will offer a fair-haired maid, her daughter, and about you draw her snares."

"Will I marry then into Gunnar's clan, and Gudrun have as wife? I'd then be well-wed if no grief lies hidden to distress me."

"Grimhild will beguile you, and ask you to fetch Brunhild for Gunnar's hand, lord of Goths; she shall easily get your promise."

"I can see that evil is before me; my will vanishes if I ask the noble maid for the hand of another, even though it is I who love her well."

"You will all swear oaths, Gunnar, Högni and you, prince, the third. Gunnar and you shall shift shapes while on the way. Gripir lies not."

"How is that? How shall we shift shapes and manner on the way? Fierce follies follow one another it seems. Explain, Gripir!"

"You take Gunnar's form, and his manners, but hold your own speech and wisdom; you shall hold to your breast the haughty fosterchild of Heimir. Nothing can prevent it."

"It seems wretched for me, Sigurd, to be called deceitful, if I do such. I would not trap with deceit for Gunnar the woman I hold to be noblest."

"Foremost of warriors, you shall sleep by the fair maid as if she were your mother. Thus your name, prince of people, shall be held high so long as men live."

"Will Gunnar, known among warriors, have that woman — tell me Gripir — though she slept beside me for three nights? Such would be strange."

"Both your weddings will be toasted together, Sigurd's and Gunnar's, in Gjuki's halls. Your shapes shift back when you come home; each regains his own mind."

"What pleasure can come of that marriage — tell me this Gripir. Will Gunnar or myself be given any happiness from it?"

"You will remember the oaths, and keep silent; you will not begrudge Gudrun's good marriage, while the fair one finds means to avenge herself."

"What will the maid accept for compensation, since we behaved deceitfully against her? She had sworn oaths with me — none fulfilled, no happiness."

"She will tell Gunnar that you have failed strong oaths which the noble prince, Gjuki's heir, trusted in."

"How is this, Gripir? Answer me. Will I be charged justly of this, or does the fair woman lie about me and herself? Explain, Gripir."

"Out of anger the strong maid deals with you, and of despair. You never dealt her harm, though the prince's maid betrayed you with intent."

"Will wise Gunnar follow Högni and Guthorm at her inciting? Will Gjuki's sons, my kinsmen, redden their sword edges?"

"Gudrun will be bitter at heart with your killers, her brothers, and never after will she be gay. Grimhild caused all this."

"Let us part now. We cannot fight our fates. You have done fairly, Gripir, what I asked of you. You have meant kindly to say fairer things of my life, if you could."

"I can console you with this, foremost war-maker, for this gift is given to your life: never will one nobler come upon this earth, under the seat of the sun, than you, Sigurd."

The Lay of Regin

Sigurd went to Hjalprek's stables and chose himself a horse, later called Grani. At that time, one of Hreidmar's sons, Regin, had come to live with Hjalprek. He was cleverer than any man, but a dwarf in stature. He was wise, cruel and skilled in magic. Regin fostered Sigurd and taught him and loved him much. He told Sigurd about his ancestors, and about the following event.

Once upon a time, Odin, Hoenir and Loki came to Andvari's Rapids; in these were many fish. Andvari was a dwarf who had lived in the rapids for a long time in the likeness of a pike, and got his food there. "One of my brothers," said Regin, "was called Otter, who often visited the rapids in the likeness of an otter. On this day he had caught a salmon and was sitting on the bank eating it with his eyes shut. Loki threw a stone at him and killed him. The gods thought they had had good-luck and skinned Otter. The same evening they sought lodging with my father, Hreidmar, and showed him their catch. We took them prisoner and demanded as a ransom that they fill the otterskin with gold and also cover the whole outside with gold. The gods sent Loki to get the gold. He went to Ran, borrowed her net and then went up to Andvari's Rapids. He cast the net before a pike and it jumped into the net. Then Loki said:

> "What is that fish that flees through the waves
>   But whose cunning cannot protect him?
> If you desire to save your life,
>   Fetch me Flame-of-the-Rhine."

> "Andvari am I, Oin was my father,
>   Over many falls I have fared;
> It was fated by a Norn in far-off days
>   That I should wade in the waters."

> "Say, Andvari, if you desire to live
>   A life in human halls,
> What is the punishment appointed for men
>   That hew each other with words?"

"Dire is the punishment appointed for men,
   They must wade in grief through Vadgelmir:
Lying words will lead men out
   On to branches that then break."

Andvari brought Loki the gold, but tried to keep one ring for himself. Loki took it from him. The dwarf went into his stone and said:

"The red gold that Gust owned
To two brothers shall bring death,
Cause harm to eight nobles,
His great treasure will do good to none."

The gods filled the otterskin with gold and set it upright. Then, as agreed, they piled up gold to cover the outside. But Hreidmar said that he could still see one grey hair and demanded that it be covered. Then Odin drew from his arm the ring Andvaranaut and covered the hair.

Loki said:

"Here is the gold, you have gotten indeed
   A huge price for our heads:
A fair fortune is not fated for your son;
   It will be the death of you both."

Hreidmar said:

"Gifts you have given, but not gifts of love,
   Not from a whole heart:
I would soon have lifted your lives from you,
   Had I foreseen your hate."

"One thing is worse; it is worse when kinsmen
   Go to war for a woman:
Of the unborn boar-warriors
   One shall hate that way."

Hreidmar said:

"I think I shall rule the red gold,
   (Said Hreidmar) as long as I live:
Little I fear your fierce threats;
   Go hence to your homes."

Fafnir and Regin demanded their share of the weregild for their
brother Otter. Hreidmar refused. So, when his father was asleep,
Fafnir struck him with a sword. Hreidmar called out to his
daughters.

> "Lyngheid! Lofnheid! My life is ended,
> Many are the woes of men."

Lyngheid said:

> "Though their father fall, few sisters
> Will visit vengeance on brothers."

Hreidmar said:

> "I wish you a daughter, a wolf-hearted maiden,
> If you get no son by the great prince:
> This maid you shall give to a man in need,
> And *their* son then will take thought how to hurt you."

Then Hreidmar died, and Fafnir took all the gold. Regin asked for
his share of the inheritance, but Fafnir refused to give him
anything. Regin asked his sister, Lyngheid, what he should do to
get his share. She said:

> "Approach peacefully and speak to him
> Gently of what is just:
> Fafnir is your brother, it befits you not
> To use the speech of swords."

This was the story that Regin told Sigurd. Then, one day, Sigurd
came to Regin's house. Regin welcomed him and said:

> "See where Sigurd sits in our hall,
> Sigmund's son, savage in battle,
> Greater in mood than a grown warrior,
> A hungry wolf, war-bent.

> "The son of Yng now sits among us,
> The mightiest prince upon Middle-Earth;
> The threads of his fate enfold all lands;
> I shall feed and foster the fearless boy."

After that Sigurd was constantly in Regin's company. Regin told him that Fafnir had taken the shape of a dragon and now lay on Gnitaheath. He had a Terror-Helm of which all living things were terrified. Regin forged for Sigurd a sword named Gram. It was so sharp that when he thrust it into the Rhine and let a tuft of wool float down the stream it cut the tuft asunder as if it had been water. With this sword Sigurd cleft Regin's anvil in half. Then Regin egged Sigurd on to attack Fafnir. But Sigurd said:

> "Eylimi's killers, Hunding's sons
> Would laugh loud and leer at a prince
> Who would rather seek for red gold
> Than seek vengeance for his father's death."

King Hjalprek gave Sigurd a fleet to avenge his father. They ran into a great storm and took shelter under a certain promontory. On the mountain stood a man who said:

> "Who ride here on Raevil's horses,
> On the foaming flood, the fierce waves?
> Soaked in sweat are the sail-horses,
> The wind is too strong for the wave-mares."

Regin answered:

> "We are here with Sigurd on the sea-trees,
> This gale, if it can, will carry us to death;
> Billows break over the beak of the ship;
> On rush the roller-steeds: who is calling?"

> "I was Hnikar of yore when young Völsung
> Gladdened ravens and gave battle;
> Now Man-of-the-Mountain you might name me,
> Or Feng or Fjölnir. I shall fare with you now."

They steered to the shore. The stranger came aboard, and immediately the storm was stilled. Sigurd said:

> "Tell me, Hnikar, about two things,
>   Of omens good and evil:
> Which are best when to battle one goes,
>   Most lucky for sweeping swords?"

Hnikar said:
>"If known to men, there are many good
>   Omens of Odin and men:
>It bodes well if black ravens
>   Fare forth with the warrior.

>"It is also good if, having left
>   Your hall for the high road,
>You should behold two heroes standing
>   Praise-eager on the path.

>"It is also good if you hear a wolf
>   Howling beneath an ash-bough:
>Whenever warriors see wolves about
>   Good fortune will befall them.

>"It is not good to go into battle
>As the moon's sister sets in the evening:
>The victors in combat have keen eyesight,
>March in wedges, are whetted to sword-play.

>"It bodes misfortune if your feet stumble
>   When about to go into battle:
>Evil ghosts are on either side,
>   Who wish to see you wounded.

>"Combed and washed should each keen one be
>   And early have eaten his fill:
>None can foretell what the night will bring;
>   It is ill to fall before omens."

A great battle took place between Sigurd and Hunding's sons,
Lyngvi and his brothers. Sigurd slew them all. Then Regin said:

>"With a bitter blade is the blood-eagle
>Carved in the back of Sigmund's killer:
>Who is bolder than the heir of the leader,
>Who has gladdened ravens and reddened the
>   earth?"

Sigurd journeyed home to Hjalprek. Once again, Regin egged him
on to attack Fafnir.

The Death of Fafnir

Sigurd and Regin went up to Gnitaheath and discovered the track of Fafnir where he slithered to the water. Sigurd dug a great pit across the path and hid in it. When Fafnir crawled from his gold heap he spewed poison which fell down on to Sigurd's head, but as he slithered over the pit Sigurd struck him to the heart with his sword. Fafnir trembled and flailed with head and tail. Sigurd leapt from the pit, and the two looked at each other. Fafnir spoke.

> "Boy, boy, whose boy are you?
>   Who are your kith and kin,
> Who so fiercely now into Fafnir's heart
>   Have plunged your bright blade?"

Sigurd hid his name because in the old days it was believed that the word of a doomed man had great power if he could cause harm to his enemy with his name. He said:

> "Noble-beast is my name, I was never born
>   To any human mother:
> I have no mother, I have no father,
>   I walk in this world alone."

> "If you have no mother, if you have no father
>   How did you enter this world?"

> "My family name is unknown to you,
>   And I myself am the same:
> Sigmund was my father, Sigurd am I
>   Who have slain you now with my sword."

> "Who urged you on, by whom were you driven
>   To do Fafnir to death?
> Bright-eyed boy, you had a biting father:
>   Courage is quick to appear."

> "My own heart urged me, my own hand drove me,
>   My own sword gave me help:
> Few who live long lives are brave
>   If cowards at an early age."

"If you ever live to grow up among friends
   I foresee you brave in battle:
But now you are a captive, caught on the field;
   It is told that all prisoners tremble."

"Why taunt me, Fafnir? Though far from home,
   Far from my father's land,
I am no captive, though caught in battle,
   Free is the life I lead."

"You take all I say as said out of hatred,
   Though I only tell the truth:
The singing hoard, the ember-red gold,
   These rings will doom you to death."

"A hoard of gold should every warrior
   Possess till the day of his death:
For man is mortal and must when fate
   Calls him go hence to Hel."

"You shall know before the ness what the Norns
allot you,
   The fate of a foolish ape:
If you row in the wind, in water you will drown;
   All things are a dread to the doomed."

"Answer me, Fafnir, for all name you
   One who knows much well:
Who are the Norns who help mothers
   To bear in their time of travail?"

"Of diverse descent I deem them to be,
   Derived from no common kin,
Some from the gods, some from the elves,
   And some from Dvalin's daughters."

"Answer me, Fafnir, for all name you
   One who knows much well:
What is the field called where fierce Surt
   And the gods shall battle together?"

"Unshaped is the field where fierce Surt
    And the gods shall sate their swords:
Bifröst ruins when they ride across it,
    Their steeds must ford the stream.

"Terror-helm I wore to protect me from men,
    When I lay guarding the gold:
Measureless then was my might, it seemed;
    No man was equal to me."

"Terror-helm can protect none
    Against foes who battle fiercely:
He soon finds when the fight begins
    Others as brave as he."

"Venom I spewed on Andvari's ring,
    When I lay on Hreidmar's hoard."

"Huge worm, you hissed loudly
    And rejoiced in your jealous heart:
Greater will the feud grow among men
    For him who possesses the helm."

"I counsel you, Sigurd, if my counsel you will take,
    To ride hence home:
The singing hoard, the ember-red gold,
    These rings will doom you to death."

"Counsel you have given, but to the gold I will ride
    Where it lies hid in the heather:
While you thrash in the throes of death,
    There where Hel shall have you."

"Regin betrayed me, will betray you also,
    The bane of both of us:
Now Fafnir must leave his life behind him;
    Your might was greater than mine."

Regin was off while Sigurd fought Fafnir and returned as Sigurd
was wiping the blood from his sword. Regin said:

"Hail, Sigurd! You have seized the victory,
   Sent Fafnir hence to Hel:
Among the men on Middle-Earth
   You were born bravest of all."

"Till the sons of victory-gods are assembled together,
   None can know or tell
Who was born the bravest:
Many are brave who do not bloody their swords
   In the breathing breast of another."

"You are glad, Sigurd, to have gotten the victory,
   As you wipe off Gram on the grass:
You have fatally wounded Fafnir, my brother;
   But I, too, played a part."

"Through your counsel I came to ride
   Hither over the fells:
The gleaming worm would still guard the hoard,
   Had you not dared me to do it."

Then Regin went to Fafnir's body and cut out his heart with the
sword Ridil, and then drank the blood from Fafnir's wounds.

"Sit, now Sigurd: I will sleep, holding
   Fafnir's heart to the flames:
First I shall eat his heart and then
   Drink his dragon's blood."

"Fast you ran while I reddened Fafnir
   With this bright blade of mine,
Measuring my strength against the might of the
   worm,
   While you lay hid in the heather."

"Long would you have left him lying there,
   The old giant in the heather,
But for the sword I myself forged,
   The bright blade I gave you."

"Courage is more than the might of a sword
    In the thick of a fierce fight:
I have seen a man battle bravely although
    He fought with a blunt blade.

"It is better to be brave than a base coward
    When sword-sweats are mingled,
Better to be glad than grieve, whatever
    Fate may befall him there."

Sigurd took Fafnir's heart and roasted it on a twig. When he thought it thoroughly cooked, as the blood boiled from the heart, he touched it to see if it was done. He burned his finger, thrust it into his mouth, and as the blood of Fafnir's heart touched his tongue, he understood the speech of birds. He heard nuthatches chattering in the brush. One said:

"Blood-spattered Sigurd sits there cooking
    Fafnir's heart on the flames:
The Gainer-of-rings would gain foresight
    If he licked that life-muscle."

"There Regin lies, laying plots
    To entrap the youth who trusts him:
His words are false, he will forge in his heart
    Bale to avenge his brother."

"He should make the Old One a head shorter,
    Send him hence to Hel:
Then all the treasure would be his alone,
    The gold that Fafnir guarded."

"If the leader-of-men would listen to us,
    Take heed of our wise warnings,
He would guard himself and gladden ravens:
    He has the ears of a wolf."

"Less wise is the leader-of-men,
    Than a battle-oak ought to be,
If he leaves Regin alive now
    After doing his brother to death."

"Unwise is the hero if his hand spares
   His foe and folk-killer:
Regin the traitor will betray him again:
   He cannot see his deceit."

"He should make Ice-Cold a head shorter,
   Rob him of all his rings:
Then all the treasure would be his alone,
   The gold that Fafnir guarded."

"Regin's fate is not rich enough
   To endure my word of death:
After his brother my blade shall quickly
   Send him hence to Hel."

Sigurd hacked off Regin's head and ate Fafnir's heart, then drank the blood of both Regin and Fafnir. Then he heard the nuthatches speak.

"Sigurd, put on the ember-red rings:
To flinch in fear is not fitting to princes.
I know of a maiden, most beautiful
And endowed with gold if you dare to win her.

"Green ways lead to the land of Gjuki:
Let fate lead forth the folk-leader;
That great king has begotten a daughter,
A bride, Sigurd, you can buy with gold.

"A high hall stands on Hindfell,
Ringed all about with blazing fires:
Brave heroes built it there,
Undark it is, a dreadful radiance.

"There, stabbed by a sleep-thorn, sleeps a valkyrie
And over her plays the peril-of-branches:
It was Ygg who did this, for she dared to feel
Another warrior than the one he desired.

"Where Vingskornir rode from the rough battle,
Sigrdrifa under her helmet lies:
You may not arouse that maiden from sleep,
Skjöldung's son, against the say of the Norns."

Sigurd rode along Fafnir's spoor to his lair and found it open.
The door and posts were iron as were all the beams in the house,
and all was buried deep in the earth. Sigurd found a great deal of
gold with which he filled two chests. He took the Terror-Helm, a
golden byrnie, the sword Hrotti, and many things of value. These
he loaded on Grani, but the horse would not move forward until
Sigurd, too, climbed on to his back.

The Lay of Sigrdrifa

Sigurd rode up to Hindfell and headed south towards Frankland. On the mountain he saw a bright light like a fire burning and shining up to heaven. But when he arrived he found a shield-wall and over it a banner. Sigurd went to the shield-wall and saw a man in full armour lying asleep. He took the helmet from his head, whereupon he saw that it was a woman. The byrnie was stuck fast as if it had grown into her flesh. With his sword Grani he slit the byrnie through from the neck down and through both sleeves, and removed it from her. She awoke, sat up and said:

> "Who has slit my byrnie and from sleep roused me,
> Who has broken the spell that bound me so long?"

> "Sigmund's son, Sigurd, who lately
> Killed the Raven's Carrion-Tree."

> "Long have I slept, long was I sleeping,
>   Long are the miseries of men:
> Odin chose to charm me to sleep
>   When he spoke a spell over me."

Sigurd sat down and asked her her name. She took a horn full of mead and gave him a remembrance drink.

> "Hail, Day! Hail, Sons of Day!
>   Hail Night and New Moon!
> With unangry eyes look hither and grant us
>   Victory while we live.

> "Hail Gods! Hail Goddesses!
>   Hail bountiful Earth!
> Grace us both with the gift of speech
>   And leech-hands while we live."

Her name was Sigrdrifa, meaning Victory-Granter, and she was a valkyrie. She said that two kings had fought. One was named Helm-Gunnar; he had grown old but was still the greatest of warriors, and to him Odin had decreed victory. The other was Agnar, Hauda's brother, who never had hopes of being favoured. Victory-Granter felled Helm-Gunnar in battle. In revenge Odin pricked her with a sleep-thorn and said that she should never thereafter fight for victory but should be married. "But", she said to him, "I in my turn bind myself by a vow to marry no man except one who knows no fear." Sigurd asked her to make her wisdom known to him, since she had knowledge of all the worlds. Sigrdrifa said:

"Apple-tree-of-battle-dins, I bring you mead
 Mixed with might and glory,
Potent with spells and pleasure-runes,
 With songs and consoling charms.

"Victory-runes, if victory you desire,
 You must etch on the hilt of your sword,
Runes on the sheath, runes on the blade,
 And twice invoke Tyr.

"Ale-runes you should know, that another's wife
 Whom you trust may not betray you:
On the back of your hands, on your horn scratch them,
 And mark on your nails *Need*.

"Thor's sign you should make on the mead-horn,
 And cast a leek in the cup:
Then I know it will never be poisoned,
 No drink can endanger your life.

"Help-runes you should know if you would help loosen
 The child from the woman's womb:
Mark them on her hands, take hold of her wrists,
 And invoke the aid of the elves.

"Sea-runes you should know to save from wreck
   Sail-steeds on the sea:
Carve them on the bow and the blade of the rudder,
   Etch them with fire on the oars;
Though high the breakers and blue the waves.
   You shall sail safe into harbour.

"Limb-runes you should know, if a leech you would
   be,
   Who can properly probe wounds:
It is best to carve them on the bark of trees
   Whose limbs lean to the east.

"Speech-runes you should know, so that no man
   Out of hatred may do you harm:
These you shall wind, these you shall fold,
   These you shall gather together,
When the people throng to the Thing to hear
   Just judgements given.

"Thought-runes you should know, if you would be
   thought by all
   The wisest of mortal men:
Hropt devised them, Hropt scratched them,
   Hropt took them to heart
From the wise waters, the waters then run
   From the head of Heidraupnir,
From the horn of Hoddrofnir.

"On the ben he stood with Brimir's sword,
   A helmet upon his head:
Then Mimir's head uttered for the first time
   Words of great wisdom.

"He spoke runes on the shield that stands before the
   shining god,
In the ear of Early-Awake and on the hoof of
   All-Wise,
On the wheel that turns ever under Hrungnir's
   chariot,
On the sled-straps and on Sleipnir's teeth.

"On the bear's paw and on Bragi's tongue,
On the wolf's foot and on the falcon's beak,
On the bloody wings and at the bridge's end,
On the palm of child-loosener and the path of
    comfort.

"On glass and on gold and the foreguesses of men,
In wine and in malt and in the mind's seat,
On Gungnir's point and on Grani's breast,
On the nails of the Norns and the Night-owl's beak.

"All were scratched off which were scratched on,
    Mingled with holy mead
    And sent on the wide ways,
Some to gods, some to elves,
    Some to the wise Vanes,
    Some to the sons of men.

"There are beech-runes, there are birth-runes,
    And all the ale-runes,
    Precious runes of power!
Unspoiled they are, unspilled they are,
    Learn them and use them long
    Till the high powers perish.

"Now you shall choose, for the choice is given you,
    Maple-of-well-forged-weapons,
Speech or silence, you shall say which:
    Evil is allotted to all."

"I shall not flee, though fated to die,
    For never have I known fear:
Grant me but this, give me all
    Your love-counsel while I live."

"I counsel you first; among kinsmen remain
    Free from fault and reproach:
Be slow to wrath though they wrong you much,
    This will do you good in death.

"I counsel you second; swear no oath
  But what you mean to abide by:
A halter awaits the word-breaker,
  Villainous is the wolf-of-vows.

"I counsel you third; at the Thing never bandy
  Words with unwise men,
For the unwise man often speaks
  Worse words than he knows.

"But speak your mind; of the silent it is often
  Believed they are low-born cowards,
  That their foes are speaking the truth .
Famous-at-home may fail abroad
  When strangers test his truth:
The reward of the liar is not long in coming;
  He dies the very next day .

"I say to you fourth ; if a sorceress dwell,
  A witch, by the way-side,
It is better to leave than to be her guest,
  Though night fall on your faring.

"Fore-sighted eyes need the sons of men
  Whenever they come to combat;
By the broad road may sit bale-wise women
  Who blunt both blades and courage.

"I counsel you fifth; though fair be the maids
  On the benches within the hall,
Let your sleep not be ruled by the silver of marriage,
  Nor beguile the girls with kisses.

"I counsel you sixth; if you sit with warriors
  And the ale-talk turns ill,
Bandy no words with bragging drunkards:
  Wine steals the wits of many.

"Quarrels and ale have often been
　　The cause of ill to heroes:
Death to some, to some bewitchment,
　　Many are the griefs of men.

"I counsel you seventh; if you come to disputing
　　With fierce-hearted fighters,
To battle is better than to be burned in the hall,
　　Although it gleam with gold.

"I counsel you eighth; of evil beware,
　　Of charming smiles of deceit:
Let no maidens entice you, nor men's wives,
　　Nor lead them into lawless pleasures.

"I counsel you ninth; cover the dead
　　Whenever on earth you find them,
Be they dead of sickness, or drowned in the river,
　　Or warriors slain by weapons.

"Dead corpses you should clean with water,
　　Wash their hands and heads,
Comb and dry them, in their coffins lay them,
　　And bid them a blessed sleep.

"I counsel you tenth; trust not ever
　　The words of a wolf's kin,
　　If you have killed his kin
　　Or felled his father:
　　Wolf's-bane is in his blood
　　Though he be glad of your gold.

"Anger and hate are ever awake,
　　So is harm also:
The boar-visored, when vain-glorious,
　　Lack both wit and weapons.

"I counsel you eleventh; there lurks evil
　　Round each bend of the road:
A long life you must not look to have,
　　So great are the hatreds grown."

The Great Lay of Sigurd

Högni   "What has Sigurd done, what dire wrong?
Why should you take the warrior's life?"

Gunnar   "Oaths Sigurd swore to me,
Solemn oaths, all belied;
He has betrayed his troth to me,
Broken faith, been false to his word."

Högni   "Brunhild has been your bane, Gunnar,
Whetting your vengeance to work this harm;
She begrudges Gudrun her good match,
And resents even more her marriage to you."

Some broiled the wolf, some sliced the worm,
Someone gave Guthorm a portion,
Before they dared to do this murder,
Lay violent hands on the valiant prince.

"Sigurd was killed south of the Rhine.
From a bough a raven raucously cried:
"Atli's sword-edge will soon be reddened,
He will kill all your kin because of your oaths."

Without stood Gudrun, Gjuki's daughter,
These words then she spoke:
"Where is Sigurd? What delays him?
Why is he not with you, my kinsmen?"

Only Högni would answer that:
"With swords we have hewn Sigurd to pieces;
Grani droops by the dead king."

Then said Brunhild, Budli's daughter:
"Enjoy well your weapons and lands;
Sigurd would soon have been sole ruler,
Had he lived longer. You are lords now."

"It was not right he should rule so
Gjuki's land and the Goth folk,
That he should have fathered five sons,
Who long for battle and to lead the host."

One laugh, wild with joy,
Brunhild gave — the beams shook.
"May you long enjoy your lands and thanes.
Having brought low the bold leader."

Then said Gudrun, Gjuki's daughter:
"You make boast of monstrous things.
May demons take Gunnar who brought death to
    Sigurd:
Wicked thoughts shall be well repaid."

The evening passed; much ale was drunk,
All of them soon grew soft-spoken,
And soon all were alseep in their beds;
Gunnar alone still lay awake.

His foot twitched, he was full of forebodings,
The destroyer-of-hosts started to ponder
On what from their boughs both birds had said,
The raven and eagle as they rode back.

Brunhild awoke, Budli's daughter,
Spirit of the Skjöldungs, steady before dawn:
"Urge me on to utter my sorrow,
Or hold me back — the harm is done."

All were silent when they heard these words:
Few could see how the same woman
Could so weep for the same deed
She had laughingly egged men on to do.

Brunhild   "I have dreamed, Gunnar, of grim things,
Of a cold hall, a cold bed,
And of you riding, a wretched king,
Your feet fettered, your foes about you.
In all the Niflungs, the oath-breakers
Your strength shall fail, false that you were.

"Don't you remember what you did, Gunnar?
How you mingled your bloods in brotherhood?
Ill have you paid him for all that,
Envious of him who was always foremost.

"It was proved then when the prince rode
Boldly off to ask for me
In what manner the mighty Gunnar
Kept his oath to kingly Sigurd.

"The beloved king had laid between us
The wound-wand, wound with gold;
The blade's edge was etched with fire,
Its flat with drops of deadly venom."

In this lay about the death of Sigurd it is told that they killed him in the open. But some say they killed him indoors while asleep in his bed. The Germans say they killed him in the woods. In the Old Lay of Gudrun, it is said that Sigurd and the sons of Gjuki rode to the Thing where he was slain. But all are unanimous in saying that they betrayed his trust and killed him while he was lying down and defenceless.

The First Lay of Gudrun

Gudrun sat watch over the dead Sigurd. She did not weep as other women do, but she was at the point of bursting from sorrow. Men and women both tried to cheer her, but it was not easy. It is said that Gudrun had eaten of Fafnir's heart and that she knew the speech of birds. This is a story of Gudrun:

Long ago Gudrun longed to die
As by Sigurd's side she sat grieving:
She wept not, nor wailed either,
Nor flailed with her hands like other women.

The wisest of earls all gathered
To give her counsel and consolation:
Gudrun's grief was too great for tears,
Her mood heavy, her heart broken.

Their wives also went to her,
Adorned with gold, to Gudrun's side:
Each one spoke of her own woe,
The bitterest sorrow suffered by each.

First spoke Gjaflaug, Gjuki's sister:
"I have lost all I love, unluckiest of women,
Three daughters, three sisters, five husbands,
Eight brothers; I am all alone."

Gudrun's grief was too great for tears,
Sick with sorrow she sat there,
Numb of heart by the hero's body.

Then spoke Herborg, Hunland's Queen:
"I have worse woes to tell of.
My seven sons besides my husband
Were slain in battle in the south-lands.

"My father, my mother, my four brothers
Were drowned when a gale made grim the sea
And the bulwarks of their ship were beaten in .

By myself I honoured them, by myself I buried them
And laid them out for their Hel-Journey.
All this I suffered in six months.
So that no man sought my love.

"Soon after, in the same year,
As a battle-trophy I was taken captive,
Compelled to dress and do up the shoes,
Bondmaid to the wife of the warrior leader.

"Out of jealousy she uttered threats,
Buffeted and beat me often:
No better house-lord have I ever found,
None worse among wives of households."

Gudrun's grief was too great for tears,
Sick with sorrow she sat there,
Numb of heart by the hero's body.

Then spoke Gullrönd, Gjuki's daughter:
"You are famed for your wisdom, my foster-mother,
But your words cannot comfort her grief.
Let us uncover the corpse of the hero."

Sigurd's shroud she swiftly removed
And neared his cheek to the knees of his wife:
"Look at your beloved, and lay now
Your lips on his as on a living king."

One glance Gudrun took,
Beheld the blood-clotted hair of her lord,
The bright eyes of the host-leader,
The sword-wounds in the warrior's breast.

Then Gudrun sank beside the body,
Her hair fell loose as she leaned on the pillow,
And her tears ran down like drops of rain.

Gudrun wept, Gjuki's daughter,
Tears flowed through her hair and on to her knees,
And the geese in the yard yelled back,
The beautiful birds bred by the maiden.

Then spoke Gullrönd, Gjuki's daughter:
"Of all women who walk the earth,
Yours, Gudrun, was the greatest love.
Outdoors or in you only loved
Life for Sigurd's sake, I know."

Then spoke Gudrun, Gjuki's daughter:
"By the sons of Gjuki my Sigurd was
As the garlic-spear over growths of weeds,
As a shining stone set in a ring,
A glittering gem of great princes.

"I fancied myself among the folk-warriors
Higher than any of Herjan's beauties;
To a little leaf in a laurel-wood
I am lessened beside the lifeless hero.

"Both at board and in bed I miss
My speech-friend: the faithless have triumphed.
Grim was the deed of Gjuki's sons,
So that with sorrow their sister weeps.

"As you were false to the oaths you swore,
So may your land lose its people.
No gain, Gunnar, shall gold be,
Those bright rings shall bring you death,
These arm-rings on which you swore oaths to Sigurd.

"Great was the joy in the garth that day,
The day when my Sigurd saddled Grani
And rode off to ask for Brunhild:
But evil befell him, ill-luck."

Then spoke Brunhild, Budli's daughter:
"May she lack both man and children,
The woman who bid you weep, Gudrun,
And gave you speech-runes in the grey of morning."

Then spoke Gullrönd, Gjuki's daughter:
"Be silent, much-hated-one. Say no more.
A bane to the noble you have been always,
Shaped for evil all men deem you,
A sore sorrow to seven kings
And to all women the worst friend."

Then spoke Brunhild, Budli's daughter:
"It was Budli's son, my brother Atli,
Who alone brought this bane to all.

"When we saw in the hall of the Hunnish people
The bed-flame-serpent about the king.
Heavy the price I paid for that journey ,
Those sights henceforth I shall see forever."

Gathering her strength, she stood by the pillar,
The maiden Brunhild, Budli's daughter;
Her eyes blazed with baleful fire
When she saw the sword-wounds in Sigurd's breast.

After that, Gudrun took the highway through wood and wilderness and travelled all the way to Denmark, where she stayed with Thora, Hakon's daughter, for three and a half years. Brunhild did not wish to survive Sigurd. She had her eight thralls and her five bondmaids killed, and then took a sword and killed herself, as is told in the Short Lay of Sigurd.

The Short Lay of Sigurd

Long ago, the young war-tested Völsung, Sigurd, sought Gjuki's court. Two brothers, wolfish warriors, swore oaths to him. He took their pledged words.

They offered him much treasure, and for wife the young Gudrun, Gjuki's daughter. For many days young Sigurd and the sons of Gjuki drank and talked together.

Then, with Sigurd, the young battle-brave Völsung, in their company, they rode to ask for Brunhild. Sigurd would have had her for himself, if he knew how.

This prince from the south lay a naked sword with damasked edge between them. The Hun neither kissed the maid nor held her in his arms; and he gave her over to the sons of Gjuki.

She felt no wrong, nor could she see in her future any coming injury. She had no faults, nor thought of fault — yet a grim future was to pass between them.

In the evening she sat alone and spoke to herself in plain words: "I shall have Sigurd, the young warrior, in my arms, or die.

"I have said what I shall regret. Gudrun is his wife, I am Gunnar's. The ugly Norns shape us to suffer long."

Often, in the evenings, she wandered about over ice and glacier with evil thoughts, as Sigurd and Gudrun went to their bed, the Hun prince wrapped his wife in fine linen and made love to her.

"I walk joyless and manless; with grim thoughts I must comfort myself."

From evil thoughts she incited herself to murder: "You, Gunnar, will lose my land and my body. With you as my lord I can never enjoy life.

"I will go back to where I was, with my kinsmen and my friends. There I will sit and pass my life away unless you have Sigurd slain and become yourself highest of warriors.

"Like father, like son. One should not keep a young wolf too long. So long as the son lives no settlement will make the vengeance less certain."

Gunnar was angry and sorrowful; he turned it over in his mind, and sat about all day. He had no idea of what would be best to do, what would be fittest. Of all, he himself was most indebted to the young Völsung, and he would feel much the loss of Sigurd.

He thought long hours about one thing or another. For a queen to leave her kingdom was unseemly in those days. He asked Högni for counsel, for he held him in full trust.

"Brunhild, born of Budli, fairest of women, is most precious to me. I would sooner lose my life than the treasure of that maid.

"Would you, for payment, betray that prince? It would be good to rule the Rhine gold, a pleasure to dispense such treasure and enjoy it, sitting in peace."

Högni knew the proper answer to that: "We should not together do such that with sword we destroy sworn oaths and trust pledged with sworn oaths.

"While the battle-bold Hun lives and we four rule over the folk, no people on earth are so blessed, nor will there be a mightier clan on earth if we foster five sons for long and our good family increase.

"I know how things stand; Brunhild's deceptions are strong."

"We can make our witless younger brother Guthorm do the fighting. He was far from our sworn oaths and trust pledged."

The reckless youth was easy to egg to it; his sword reached to Sigurd's heart.

Bravely, Sigurd took revenge in the hall and struck at the reckless youth. Gram flew with force to Guthorm, bright iron impelled by the prince's hand.

He felled his foe in two pieces; hand and head fell one way, his legs fell down in place.

Gudrun, carefree, had been asleep in bed beside Sigurd. But her joy fled when she awoke flooded with the blood of the friend of Frey.

She thrashed out with her arms, but the brave-hearted one rose beside her in bed: "Cry not so sorely Gudrun, my beautiful bride; your brothers still live.

"My heir is too young to escape his enemies' house. They have acted on rash counsel, darkly and foolishly.

"Had I seven nephews they would never ride to the Thing. I know now quite well what is happening. Brunhild alone has ruled this evil.

"That maid loved me before all men, yet I never worked ill against Gunnar. I kept my sworn oaths and my marriage vows, lest I be called his wife's lover."

Gudrun cast out a cry, and the prince his life. She thrashed so wildly with her hands that the drinking cups in the corner rattled and the geese in the yard cried back.

Then Brunhild laughed, Budli's daughter, just once from her heart, as she heard from her bed the weeping of Gjuki's daughter.

Gunnar, hawk-taming warrior, spoke: "Vengeance-hungry woman, do not laugh, happy in the hall, for any good. Why has your fair colour left you, nurturer of ill? I think you are fey.

"For this deed you are worthy to have your brother Atli cut down by us before your eyes, to see his bloody sores and bleeding wounds for you to bandage."

"No one reproaches you, Gunnar, though you have killed enough. Atli little fears your wrath; he will live longer than you and shall always bear greater strength.

"I remind you Gunnar — and you know it — that you first started this affair. I was young and carefree, surrounded by wealth in my brother's hall.

"Nor did I want any man to possess me before you Gjukungs rode to court, you three folk-kings on horse. Had the journey never been!

"I pledged myself to the folk-king who sat with gold on Grani's back. He was not like you in his eyes, or in any part of his being — though you think yourselves kings of the folk.

"But Atli said to me that he would not share gold or land unless I have myself married, nor could I hold a part of the treasures which were given to me when I was young, the money doled out to me as a child.

"Then my thoughts turned every way: should I, bold in my byrnie, battle and kill, against my brother's sake. I decided then to be grief to many men, and famous in it.

"We let loose true words: my mind was bent on getting treasure, rings of red gold, from Sigmund's son; I wished no other man's wealth.

"I loved one, no other; I never had woman's fickle heart. After he learns of my death Atli will know all this.

"I will not, like a weak-minded woman, lead another man; so for my woe comes vengeance."

Gunnar, king of the folk, rose up and laid his arms about the maid's neck; one after another, from their hearts, went to hold her back.

She thrust all of them from her neck. No one would stay her from her long journey.

Gunnar took Högni aside to speak: "I will have all my men go into the hall with yours — there is much need — to see if they can stop Brunhild's death journey; in time some other hindrance will come, so let us do what is necessary."

Högni knew the proper answer to that: "Let no one hold her from her long journey, so she may never be born again. Luckless she came from her mother's knee, was born always to wickedness, and to many men a heartbreak."

Gunnar turned sadly from the talk to where Brunhild was giving out her goods.

She looked over all her possessions, her hall-women and serving girls dying. She put on a gold byrnie — ill was in her heart — before she thrust in the sword point.

She sank to one side on a pillow and, wounded by blade, thought of her counsel:

"Now come all who wish the least gold to get. I have to each a fashioned garment, fabric, and coloured cloth, bright clothes."

Everyone was silent and thought of her counsel, and all together knew the proper response. "Enough die, we wish yet to live. Hall women do not win honour so."

Then the wise woman, young of years, clad in linen, spoke these words: "I would not have unwilling or timid men lose their lives for my sake.

"But few treasures will burn on your bones when you die, nor will you follow me with Menja's wealth.

"Sit down, Gunnar. I will speak with you of the bright maid. I am past hope of life. Your ships will not all be on the sea when I have breathed my last.

"Make peace with Gudrun sooner than you would. With the prince, the dead warrior, that maid has a dreary keepsake.

"The mother bears child, a daughter is born. She, Swanhild, will be brighter than the clearest day, brighter than the sun's ray.

"Give Gudrun to a good warrior, a foe of many men. She may not be happy in the choice. Atli will come to have her, my brother born of Budli.

"I remember much of how I was treated when sorrowful fraud was worked on me; I was joyless while I lived.

"You will want to take Oddrun, but Atli will prevent you; you will meet in secret; she will love you as I should have if we had been fated well.

"Atli will mistreat you; will place you in peril, lay you in the serpent-pit.

"No longer will he live for it, but Atli lose his life, his fortune, and the lives of his sons, for Gudrun, with cruel heart, will stain his bed with a sharp sword.

"It would be better for our sister Gudrun to follow the death of her first husband, if good counsel be given her or her heart been as mine.

"I speak slowly now; she will not lose her life for my sake. High waves will carry her to Jonak's noble land.

"There she will bear babies, guardians of heritage, Jonak's sons. She will send Swanhild, hers and Sigurd's daughter, from the land.

"Bikki's counsel will bite her, for Jörmunrek lives for no good; Gudrun's tears are the more, for all of Sigurd's race have perished.

"I ask a boon of you that will be my last request in this world: make a wild pyre on the plain so that there will be equal space under all of us who died with Sigurd.

"Deck the pyre with shield and cloth, Gaulish cloth well-dyed, and many Gaulish things. Burn me by the side of the Hun prince.

"Burn by the side of the Hun prince my servants honoured with treasures, two at the head, and two hawks. Then all is divided equally.

"Lay the ringed sword between us, as the sharp-edged iron once lay when we two climbed into one bed and promised to be husband and wife.

"Never will the hinges of the door with coloured rings fall on his heel then, if my bondsmen follow him from here. Our journey will not be lowly.

"Five bondmaids, eight servants of good birth, my fosterer, and the dowry which Budli gave his daughter will follow him.

"Much I have said, more I would have if the ruler of fate had granted more time. My voice fails, my wounds swell, I have spoken the truth — so I die."

Brunhild's Hel-Ride

After the death of Brunhild, two pyres were laid: one for Sigurd,
which was ignited first; on the other, Brunhild was burnt, atop a
hearse covered with a rich cloth. It is told how Brunhild rode the
hearse down the Hel-way, and passed the house of a giantess.

"Depart! You shall not pass through
My tall gates of towering stone:
It befits a wife to wind yarn,
Not to know another's husband.

"To what end, woman from Gaul,
False of heart, would you enter my realm?
Fair woman, if you want the truth,
You have bathed your hands in the blood of men."

"Bar me not, bride of stone-elves!
They think me the higher, those who know
Both our births, better than you."

"You were born, Brunhild, Budli's daughter,
Of all women the worst fated,
Brought sorrow and death to the sons of Gjuki,
Down to nothing their noble house."

"I shall tell you, giantess, joyless news,
News of the worst, if you want the truth:
Gjuki's sons by guile made me
A loveless bride, a breaker of oaths.

"Hild-under-helm they all called me,
All who knew me in Hlymdale,
Where, under the oak, over eight sisters
Valfather flung feathered cloaks.
Twelve winters I knew, if you want the truth,
When I plighted my troth to the peerless warrior.

"Hjalm-Gunnar to Hell I sent,
The old Goth, when I gave victory
To young Agnar, Auda's Brother:
Angry with me was Odin for that.

"He scarfed me in shields on Skatalund,
Red and white ones, their rims interlocked,
With a sleep-spell bound me, and bade tree-foe
Burn all about the bed where I lay.

"Then the hero, the thane who never
Had felt fear, through the flames rode
To fetch thence Fafnir's hoard
And rouse me at last from my long sleep.

"On Grani he rode, the gold-sharer,
To the hall where my foster-father ruled:
In the king's host, he was counted best,
Viking of the Danes, most valiant of all.

"In a single bed we slept and were happy:
As if we had been brother and sister,
Neither laid a lustful hand
Upon the other for eight nights.

"Then Gjuki's daughter, Gudrun, mocked me,
Said I had slept in Sigurd's arms:
I found then, what I fain would have not,
That through a trick I had taken a husband.

"Men and women on Middle-Earth
Must contend with grief and for too long:
Never shall Sigurd be sundered from me;
None shall unjoin us. Giantess, yield!"

The Second Lay of Gudrun

A maid among maids my mother raised me,
Bright in a bower with brothers I loved,
Till the day when Gjuki adorned me with rings,
With gold adorned me and gave me to Sigurd.

Sigurd beside the sons of Gjuki
Was a green leek among grown weeds,
Or a high-born hart over humble beasts,
Or ember-red gold over grey silver.

Envious, though, were the thoughts of my brothers
Because my man was more mighty than they:
They could not rest, they could not sleep
Till they saw Sigurd, slain at their feet.

Riderless, Grani rode to the Thing,
There was much noise, but no Sigurd:
The saddle-beasts with blood were flecked
From their usual toil under the killers.

I went weeping, wet-cheeked,
To talk to Grani, told him to speak:
The horse bowed his head to the grass,
He knew that his master was not alive.

Long I thought, for my thoughts were divided,
Before I asked what had happened to Sigurd.

Gunnar was silent and grim, but Högni
Told me of Sigurd's sorrowful death:
"From our sword-strokes slain he lies,
Gothorm's killer, and given to the wolves.

You will find Sigurd on the southern way
Where already the raven screams,
The eagle also, hungry for carrion,
Wolves howl over your man."

"How can you wish, Högni, to say
Words of such woe, unwelcome to hear?
Would that the raven had ripped out
The heart from your breast for this ill-deed.

Högni in answer said only this —
He found it hard to find the words —
"Greater, Gudrun, your grief would be,
If the heart the raven had ripped were mine."

I turned away and went alone,
Went to the woods for the wolves' leavings:
I wept not, I wailed not,
Nor flailed with my hands like other women,
As there I sat over Sigurd's body.

Dark seemed the night, pitch-dark,
As I sat in sorrow over Sigurd's body,
Wishing only that the wolves would rend me,
Or fire burn me like birch-wood.

I journeyed from the fells for five days
Till the high halls of Half I saw.

For seven half-years I sat with Thora,
Hakon's daughter in Denmark:
In gold she broidered to give me pleasure
Danish swans and southern halls.

Together we wove the warriors at sword-play,
With cunning skill the king's thanes,
Hun heroes in helmets and bearing
Red shields, a shining host.

The ships of Sigurd, sailing from land,
Their beaks gilded, their bows carved,
Embroidered on board the brave warriors,
Sigar and Siggeir, south at Fjon.

Then Grimhild, the Gothic woman,
Learned what had happened and how I fared:
She rose from the table and told her sons
To ask themselves what they ought to do.
Who would pay the price of atonement
To satisfy the sister for the slain hero!

Gunnar was ready to give treasure
In satisfaction, so was Högni.
Then Grimhild asked them who would go
To saddle the horses, to harness the wagons
To mount the horses, let the hawks fly
And bend the strings of the bows of yew.

The valiant warriors, Valdar of the Danes,
With Jarisleif and Jariskar
And Eymod also, in they came
In visored helmets, the host of Langobards,
With short swords and short byrnies:
They had red fur coats and red-brown hair.

They offered me gifts of great price,
Precious presents and spoke their thoughts:
All of them wished to win my trust,
Many looked doleful, but I did not trust them.

Grimhild brought me a beaker to drink,
Cool and bitter to banish my cares:
It was fortified with fate's power,
With the cold sea, and with sons' blood.

There were runes on that horn of every sort,
Carved and stained, but I could not read them,
Long heather-fish from Hadding's land,
Ears of corn and entrails of beasts.

Ill-fortunes were in that beer,
Burned acorns and herbs from the woods,
Bloody bowels, boiled pig's liver,
And soot from the hearth to soothe cares.

They forgot then they had given me
Boiled meats of boar-princes:
Three kings now knelt before me,
And now Grimhild began to speak.

"I will give you, Gudrun, gold to keep,
Fine treasures that your father owned,
Hlödver's hall, ember-red rings,
All the bed-linens of the boar-prince.

"Linens woven by the women of the Huns,
Embroidered with gold to gladden your eyes:
You alone shall rule the riches of Budli,
Have much wealth and be married to Atli."

"I do not want to wed a husband
Nor with the brother of Brunhild to live:
It does not become me to increase a family
With Budli's son, nor to be content."

"Do not seek for a savage vengeance,
Though we were at fault for the first blow:
It will seem as if Sigurd and Sigmund were
Both alive if you bear sons."

"I cannot, Grimhild, be glad or merry,
Nor hope for the embraces of a brave warrior,
Since the carrion-beast and the cruel raven
So sorely drank Sigurd's blood."

"Among the folk I have found for you
The foremost of all, the highest-born:
He shall have you till age fell you,
Unless, woman, you want to be manless."

"Do not try to do this thing.
No good will come from that cursed race,
Atli will deal harm to Gunnar
And rip the heart from Högni's breast:
I will not rest till I have reaved him of life
In the prime of his days, the death-bringer."

Weeping, Grimhild grasped the words
Which boded doom to her dear sons,
And greater harms to all her line.

"Lands I will give you with their loyal peoples,
Vinbjörg shall be yours, and Valbjörg also;
You shall have them for life and be happy, daughter."

"Then from kinsmen and kings I must choose
Against my will to be wed to a man
Who will only bring me bane not joy,
The bale-of-brothers will be bale to his sons."

The brave ones mounted the backs of horses,
But the Gaulish women in wagons rode,
Seven days were carried through cold land,
Seven more sailed on the waves,
Rode seven more through mountain country.

The gates were opened by the guards on watch:
We rode into the high fortress.

Atli roused me: to him I seemed full
Of cruel thoughts about my kin's deaths.

He asked me to interpret an ill-prophecy:
"Just now the Norns awoke me;
I imagined, Gudrun, Gjuki's daughter,
That you pierced my heart with a poisoned sword."

"A dream of metal, that means fire,
Of a maid's anger, that means pride:
To ban evil I will burn you with fire
For your comfort and health, though hateful to me."

"Fresh saplings fell in my dream,
Here in the yard where I hoped to grow them,
Torn up by the roots and red with blood,
Borne to the bench and brought me to chew.

"Hawks flew from my hands in my dream,
Without prey to an ill-abode:
Their hearts with honey I had to chew,
Swollen with blood, in sorry mood.

"Hounds were loosed from my hands in my dream,
Both howling, hungry for joys:
I imagined their flesh turned foul and rotten,
And, unwilling, I had to chew them.

"Men will consider sacrifices,
And white whales worry heads,
Whales fated in a few nights
To taste their lords a little before dawn.

"I lay down, but I did not sleep:
What I thought of then, that I shall do."

Atli had a bondservant named Herkja. She had been his mistress. One day she told Atli that she had seen Thjodrek and Gudrun together. Atli was very angry. Gudrun said:

The Third Lay of Gudrun

"Why so heavy of heart, Atli, why
　　Now do you never laugh?
More seemly the thanes would think it if you
　　Spoke with men and me."

"I am grieved, Gudrun, Gjuki's daughter,
　　By the tale Herkja has told me,
That you lay with Thjodrek between linen sheets,
　　Willingly like a wife."

"I will swear oaths by the holy stone
　　That Herkja's tale is untrue:
I never slept with the son of Thjodmar
　　Willingly like a wife.

"I never embraced the boar-prince
　　Nor kissed the king of hosts;
Of other things spoke Thjodrek and I,
　　Of afflictions born by us both.

"Thjodrek came here with thirty warriors,
　　Not one is left alive:
Of brothers and byrnies both you bereft me,
　　Of all my close kin.

"Send for Saxi, the southerners' lord,
　　Let him bless the boiling cauldron.

"Gunnar comes not, I call not Högni,
　　Nor shall see my sweet brothers:
Högni would avenge my hurts with a sword;
　　I declare I am free from fault."

There were seven hundred in the hall watching
    As the queen approached the kettle.

She thrust to the bottom her bright palm,
    Brought up the holy stones:
"Look, Prince! I am proved innocent,
    Blameless by the boiling kettle."

Joyful at heart was Atli when he saw
    That Gudrun's hand was whole.
"Now Herkja shall try the test of the kettle,
    Who hoped to do Gudrun harm."

Nothing sadder had they seen who saw that,
    How Herkja's hand was scalded:
They flung the maid into a foul bog.
    Thus Gudrun got revenge.

Heidrek was the name of a king: his daughter was called Borgny.
Her lover was called Vilmund. She could not bring forth her babies
until Oddrun, Atli's sister came. Oddrun had been the mistress of
Gunnar. Gjuki's son.

Oddrun's Tears

I heard it said in old tales
How a maiden came to Mornaland;
No one the whole world over could
Find help for Heidrek's daughter.

Oddrun heard this, Atli's sister,
Heard that the maid was mortally sick:
She brought from its stall a bridled horse
And laid a saddle on the swarthy one.

Through flat fields she fared then
Till to the Huns' high hall she came;
In she went through the end door,
And threw the saddle from the slim horse.

"What is spoken of widely on earth?
What has happend in Hunland!"
"Borgny lies here in labour pains;
You, Oddrun can help your friend."

"Who among the lords has harmed her thus,
Who has brought Borgny to this?"

"Vilmund, friend of the valiant, is his name;
Between warm blankets he embraced the maid
For five winters; her father knew nothing."

That is all, I think, that they said;
Oddrun knelt by the knees of the maid,
Sang correctly, sang strongly,
Loosening charms for luckless Borgny,

That a girl and a boy might be born on earth ,
Fathered by Högni's future killer:
The sick maiden spoke at last,
Who till then had uttered no word.

"May the gracious beings grace you, Oddrun,
Frigg and Freya, and the fair gods,
For your hands have taken this evil from me."

"I had no wish to help you, Borgny,
Unworthy have you ever been;
I have performed what I am fated to do,
To help all is my heritage."

"You are mad, Oddrun, and out of your wits
To utter such words of hurt to me;
A faithful friend, I have followed you
As if two brothers had been our fathers."

"I remember well your words that evening
When I brought beer in a beaker to Gunnar.
No other maiden but me alone
Should suffer such fate, you said, thereafter."

Then the woeful woman sat down
To tell of her grief and her great bale.

"Happy was the hall where I was raised
Among boar-princes and their people's counsel.
I enjoyed for a while the wealth of my father,
For five winters, then my father died.

"On his death-bed the doleful king
Lay and spoke his last words.
He bid me be enriched with red gold
And be married in the south to the son of Grimhild.

"But the helm should go, he ordered, to Brunhild:
That maiden, he said, would be much loved,
A nobler woman would never be born,
Nobler or fairer, unless Fate destroyed her.

"Brunhild sewed at her bower table,
She ruled over peoples and rich lands.
The earth quaked and the heavens too
When Fafnir's killer came to the burg.

"With Gaulish weapons a war was fought,
And the burg broken which Brunhild had.
It was not long, just a little while,
Till Brunhild learned of their lies and deceit.

"For this she took a terrible revenge,
So that we all had hard trials:
The tale has travelled, it is told in all lands
How she killed herself beside Sigurd's body.

"Then I met Gunnar and began to love him,
The boar-prince, as Brunhild should have.

"They offered Atli ember-red rings,
Would have given great gifts to my brother
As a marriage fee, fifteen livestock
And Grani's burden which he greatly longed for.

"But Atli refused then; he refused, he said
To take gifts from Gjuki's sons.
Our desires were too strong to struggle against;
I laid myself down by the dealer-of-rings.

"Presently my kinsmen suspected our love,
Said they had often seen us together,
But Atli swore that I would never
Use guile or be guilty of vice.

"But never should a man deny such.
When desires are shared they soon prevail.

"Atli sent his servants forth
Through the dark wood to keep watch on us:
By ill-fortune they found us there,
Where in one bed, embracing, we lay.

"We offered the thanes ember-red rings
To keep silent and say nothing,
But home they sped in haste to my brother;
Unlucky the time when they told Atli,

"Gudrun had far greater right
To learn what had happened, but they hid it from her.

"Gjuki's sons upon golden hooves
Rode into the court; there were cries and shouts:
They cut the heart out of Högni's breast
And set Gunnar in the serpent pit.

"When this happened I had gone
To Geirmund to make the drink.
Gunnar struck the strings of his harp,
The king thought I would quickly come
To save the life of the illustrious one.

"I heard how his harp on Hlesey spoke
Tidings of grief and great distress.
'Make ready the boat,' I bid my maidens,
I longed to save the leader's life.

"We floated across the flood then
Until I saw all of Atli's court.

"Then Atli's mother came hobbling out,
The wretched one — she should rot away —
And into Gunnar's heart she dug.
I was too late to save the illustrious one.

"Often I have wondered how I could,
Gold-adorned one, go on living.
I had hoped to love like my own self
The bold-in-danger, the dealer-of-swords.

"You have listened while I related to you
Many ills of mine and theirs.
All men seek their desires on earth.
Oddrun's tears are over now."

Gudrun, Gjuki's daughter, avenged her brothers, as we know. She first killed the sons of Atli, then she killed Atli himself, and finally she burned the hall and all its company. About these events do these words speak.

Atli's Death

> Atli once sent a warrior to Gunnar
> Knefröd he was called: he came riding
> To Gjuki's garth; in Gunnar's hall
> They were drinking ale at the hearth-benches.

> Hiding their fears of the Hun's anger
> Brave kinsmen drank beer together:
> From his guest-seat, the southern warrior
> Called out these cold words.

> "On a champing-bit mare through Mirkwood,
> I rode on this errand at Atli's bidding:
> I was told, Gunnar, to tell you to come
> To Atli's land with your hearth-guards.

> "Shields he will give you and shafts of ash,
> Gilded helmets and Hunnish slaves,
> French-red sarks and saddle-cloths,
> And your choice of steeds that champ the bit.

> "Wide Gnitaheath he offers you too,
> Screaming spears and splendid weapons,
> Store of treasure and stallions from the Dneipr,
> And the forest that men know as Mirkwood."

> Gunnar turned to talk to Högni:
> "What is your counsel, warrior, about this?
> I know of no gold on Gnitaheath,
> Of any hoard equal to our treasure.

"Seven rooms-full of swords we have,
Every blade embossed with gold,
My horse is the swiftest, my sword the keenest,
Of my bench-decking bows, my byrnies of gold,
Each one has more worth than the wealth of the
Huns.''

"Why did our sister send us a ring
Woven with wolf's wool? A warning, I think.
A wolf's hair was wound in the ring:
Wolfish our road if we ride this errand.''

Neither his neighbours nor his kinsmen,
Nor friends nor counsellors encouraged Gunnar.
Then Gunnar spoke as a great king will,
Princely in his hall, from his proud heart.

"Rise up, Fjörnir, and hand round
The gold cups to the clan of warriors.

"The wolf will rule the realm of the Niflungs,
The old grey one, if Gunnar be lost:
Black-pelted bears will bite and rend
To gladden bitch-packs if Gunnar fall.''

Then the fierce-in-battle led his fearless household
Weeping, out of the hall of the Niflungs;
Högni's heir uttered these words:
"Fare well wherever your hearts may lead you.''

Their horses' hooves sped over the mountains,
Bit-champing mares through Mirkwood;
The Hun-forest shook as the heroes rode;
They spurred and galloped over green fields,

To Atli's land and his huge fortress,
The hall of the southerners, set with benches,
Decked about with abundance of shields
And ash-spears, where Atli drank
Ale with his men. Outside was set
A guard to warn if Gunnar should come
With screeching spears to the scathe of battle.

Inside the hall their sister met
Both her brothers — no beer had she drunk.
"You are trapped, Gunnar, by the treacherous
Huns,
You can gain nothing. Go quickly.

"Better it were, brothers, in byrnies to have come
To Atli's hall, as hearth-guardians,
To have sat in the saddle for sun-bright days,
To have made the Norns to lament a corpse
And the Shield-Maidens to shun your blades,
Brought Atli himself to the serpent-pit:
Now that worm-pit is awaiting you."

"It is too late, sister, to summon the Niflungs,
Too far to rally from our Rhine hills
The household band of brave warriors."

They seized Gunnar and set him in fetters,
King of the Burgundians, bound him fast.

Seven men Högni slew with his sword
And thrust an eighth into the hot fire.
So shall a fighter defend himself:
Högni acted as the hands of Gunnar.

They asked Gunnar, the Goth prince:
"Will you buy your life with bright gold?"

"Högni's heart in my hand must lie,
Cut from the breast of the bold rider,
With a cruel sax from the son of a prince."

They cut the heart out of Hjalli's breast,
And bore it on a trencher, bloody to Gunnar.

(Then spoke Gunnar, spear-ward of heroes,
"Here I have the heart of Hjalli the coward,
Unlike the heart of Högni the bold.
It trembles much, as it lies on the trencher,
Still it trembled more, when it stayed in his breast."

Högni laughed as his heart was cut;
The living battler thought least to cry.
Bloody on the trencher, it was borne before
Gunnar.)

Gunnar, the renowned, of the Niflungs, said:
"Here I have the heart of Högni the brave,
Unlike the heart of Hjalli the coward.
Little it trembles on the trencher now:
It trembled still less when it lay in his breast."

"Soon, Atli, soon you shall be
As far from men's eyes as from our treasure.
All belongs now alone to me,
All the hoard of the Niflungs now Högni is dead.

"There was ever doubt while Högni lived.
There is none now. Now I am alone.
The Rhine shall get the gold of heroes,
The river hold the hoard of the Niflungs.
Better it rest in rolling waters
Than shine in the hands of Hun warriors."

"Turn the waggon-wheels: fetter the warrior."
Atli mounted his mare Glaum
While kept at sword-point were the king's friends.
Then Gudrun, the great-hearted
Entered the hall but held back her tears.

"The same fate shall befall you, Atli,
For the oaths which to Gunnar of old you swore,
By Odin's holy hill you swore them,
Swore them by the sun in her southern hall,
By the horse of the bed-rests and by Ull's ring."

Horses were harnessed to haul thence,
Bound to a cart, the keeper of treasure,
Drag their prisoner to the place of death.
They cast the king into the cruel pit,
Crawling with adders, but the hero there
Stood unflinching and struck his harp.
The strings resounded. So shall a brave
Giver of rings deny gold to his foes.

Then Atli turned his earth-turning steed
And went home away from the murder.
There was clamour in the court, clatter of hoofs,
And weapon songs as his warriors returned.

Gudrun came forth to greet Atli,
A gold goblet she gave to her lord:
"Welcome home to your hall; receive
Gladly from Gudrun the Hel-going of boys."

Cups filled with the foaming ale
Rang in the hall where the Huns were gathered,
Long-bearded men on the benches together.

Bright-faced Gudrun brought out
Strong drink for the doomed warriors,
And then to Atli with hate she spoke:

"Sword-chieftain, you have chewed with relish
The bloody hearts of your own sons,
Greedily fed on the flesh of the slain.

"To your knee henceforth you shall never call
Erp or Eitil, now ale-merry,
Nor see them sitting on the high bench,
Sharing out gold of shafting spears
Or cutting the manes of the mares they ride."

Sad songs were sung then,
Heavy with sorrow, the Huns wept.
But Gudrun wept not; she wept neither
For her bear-fierce brothers or her bonny sons,
Fathered by Atli, innocent, young.

Red rings and rich gold
Swan-bright Gudrun gave her house-churls;
And fate waxed at the wish of Gudrun:
After that the temple treasure was less.

Atli, weaponless, weary with drink,
Was off his guard when Gudrun struck:
More pleasant had been their play together
When they fondly embraced before the princes.

She gave the bed his blood to drink,
Unleashed the whelps, awakened the house-churls,
And kindled fires before the doors:
Such was her weregild for her slain brothers.

The fire she set consumed all
Who had come from Mirkwood after murdering
Gunnar.
Hall-timbers fell, the temple smoked,
The home of the Budlings burned and the doomed
Shield-maidens shrivelled in the flames.

Nothing was left. Never since
Has valiant woman so avenged her brothers.
The fierce one before she died
Made a thorough end of three kings.

The Greenland Lay of Atli

Many have heard how long ago a feast of warriors which pleased none came to its end. Talk grew big, and fear came after, to Gjuki's sons as well, they who had been tricked.

The Skjöldungs' fate approached — they were doomed — but it turned out ill for Atli too, though he was cunning. As if he had toppled a pillar on himself he brought about his own harm, once he had sent a messenger to ask his kinsmen to come soon.

The mistress of the house was wise and had her wits about her as she overheard the words they spoke in secret. But she lacked the means to help them. They were to cross the sea, and she could not come.

So she shaped runes, but Vingi changed them before he delivered them, for he was bent on evil. Atli's messengers journeyed over Limfirth to where the brave heroes lived.

They were ale-friendly and kindled welcome fires, and suspected no fraud in those who had come. They received gifts of peace, hung them on a pillar and did not recognize the warning.

Kostbera, Högni's queen, an astute woman, came and greeted them both; Glaumvor, Gunnar's wife, was happy; she was wise and could serve the needs of her guests.

They invited Högni to their home, if he wished to go. If he had been alert, their treachery would have been clear. Gunnar promised to go if Högni wished. Had he been advised, Högni should have refused.

The brave heroes brought mead, there was cheer for all, drinking-horns were brought until all had fully drunk.

The couple went to their rest as they thought proper. Kostbera was shrewd, understood runes and read them by the firelight; but she guarded her tongue; the letters were unclear and she did not understand them.

She and Högni went to their bed, and her husband's beloved dreamed, and did not hide it from her brave husband as soon as she awoke.

"You are off from home, heed my advice, for few are perfectly wise. Go another time! I see these runes your sister scratched. That fair one asks you not to come now.

"One thing makes me wonder — I cannot understand it — how it happened that the clever one made errors; underneath it is hinted that you will both die if you come soon; she either missed a stave, or others changed them."

"All women are distrustful, but that is not my nature, I look for no evil, except to repay a debt. The king will give us ember-red gold. I have no fears, though we may hear of horrors."

"It will go badly with you if you go there. You'll get no hearty welcome at this time. I will not hide that I dreamed that it will pass badly for you.

"I dreamed your bedsheets burned in fire, and the flames shot up high through the house."

"Here are some linen rags lying, little thought of; they will burn soon, and those are the bedsheets you saw."

"I saw a bear enter. He broke down the pillars and shook his paws so that it frightened us. He had many of us in his mouth and we were powerless. There was more than a little panic then."

"Storms grow big and become a dread. When you think of a white bear there will be a blast from the east."

"I saw an eagle fly in from the end of the hall that hurt us. He splattered us with blood; I imagined that his fierceness was Atli's rage."

"We slaughter soon, so we see blood. Dreaming of eagles often means oxen; Atli's heart is full no matter what you dream." They spoke no more — all talk passes.

The high-born Glamuvor awoke — it was the same — and said she had dreamed of harm. Gunnar thought there were two ways to see it.

"I dreamed of a ready gallows, and you will be hanged; snakes bite at you, though I found you alive. Ragnarök was at hand. What would that mean?

"I saw a bloody sword lifted from your shirt; ill is such a dream to tell one's husband; I saw a spear sticking through you. Wolves growled at either end."

"When hounds run, one hears lots of barking. Sounds of dogs often precede flights of spears."

"I saw a river run in from the end of the hall. It spurted from the benches, roared with fury, broke the feet of you two brothers. The waters stopped for nothing; that must mean something.

"I saw dead women coming here in the night. Their clothes were wretched. They wanted to take you and invited you to their benches. I thought the friendly spirits had left you."

"It is too late to talk; all is settled. The journey is fixed. I cannot turn from the trip, though it is likely that we are short-lived."

They were eager to be off by the light of dawn. All rose, but the women wanted to hold them back. Five went together, more than half that number of house servants — that was ill-planned. Snaevar and Solar were Högni's sons and Orkning was he who followed. Happy was the queen's brother, this shield-tree.

The fair-dressed maids followed until the firth parted them. The fair ones tried to dissuade them, but they wouldn't listen.

Glaumvor, Gunnar's wife, spoke to Vingi, as she saw fit: "I do not know if you will be rewarded as we would wish, but your coming is a crime if evil follows."

Then Vingi answered without sparing himself: "May the giants take me if I lie to you, the gallows have me if I think against our truce.

Bera, happy in her heart, spoke: "Sail safely, win victory. Fare you well and no one shall deny it."

Högni answered — he held his kin dear —: "Be of good cheer, wise-ones, no matter what comes. Many speak and still lose much; advice does little to lead one home."

They looked at each other before they turned to the sea. It seemed their fates changed as their ways parted.

The strong ones rowed so that the keel half tore. They pulled with their backs, enraged. The oar-straps split, the oarlocks snapped. They turned from the boat without even making it fast.

A little later — I must tell the tale to the end — they saw Budli's home; the gate creaked when Högni struck it.

Then Vingi spoke — better had he not — "Go far from this house. You will find it treacherous. I will have you hacked down and burned. With fair words I bade you come, underneath was deceit. Or, wait apart while I cut your gallows."

Högni thought little of giving up as he heard these words. He was afraid of nothing to come. "Do not try to frighten us. You will seldom succeed. Do not say a word or your pains will be lengthened."

They struck down Vingi and dropped him to Hel. They laid their axes to him while his last breath rattled.

Atli's men rallied together and advanced in their byrnies. They marched so the court was between them. All at once they spoke in their anger: "It has long been decided to take your lives."

(Högni) "Evil it is if long planned, but you are unready, and we have struck down one, dropped him to Hel. He was of your host."

They were enraged when they heard these words. They moved fingers to grasp the cords, shot sharply and covered themselves with shields.

The news came inside of what was happening outside before the hall. They heard a thrall tell it loudly.

Gudrun was fierce when she heard the ill news. Laden with necklaces, she threw them off. She threw down her silver so the rings burst apart.

She opened the doors a little, then went out. Unafraid, she greeted the visitors. It was her last greeting as she turned to the Niflungs. She spoke the truth and would have said more:

"I sought your safety, to keep you at home; but, no one escapes fate, and you came." She spoke carefully to keep the peace, but they would not listen. They all said no.

She, born into fortune, saw their dire play, hardened her heart and cast off her cloak, took a naked sword and guarded her kinsmen's lives. She was easy in battle wherever her hand fell.

Gjuki's daughter struck down two warriors. She felled Atli's brother, aimed her stroke and cut off his foot. They bore him off.

She hewed another so he did not rise again. Her hands did not falter as she sent him to Hel.

They fought a battle widely famed, more than any other deed of Gjuki's kin. It is said of the Niflungs that, while they still lived, they shaped battle with swords, they slit byrnies, hewed helmets as their hearts urged them.

They fought most of the morn, midday passed, fought through dusk and the next dawn. The plain was flooded with blood before the fight ended. Before they fell, Bera's two boys and her brother had gained the better of eighteen.

Atli spoke. He was enraged: "It is ill to look at, all your doing. There were thirty warlike thanes. Eleven of us still live, like remnants of a fire.

"There were four brothers when we lost Budli; two lie hewn; Hel has half.

"A fine marriage I made — I cannot hide it — baleful woman. I profit nothing from you; we have had little peace since you came into my hands, deprived me of friends, tricked me out of riches, sent my sister to Hel, and this grieves me most."

"Do you speak of this, Atli. You acted first. You took my mother and killed her for her wealth, you starved my sister's daughter in a cave. Laughable it is to tell me your griefs. I thank the gods if things go ill with you."

(Atli) "I urge you on, nobles; strengthen your strokes for this grand wife. Do your best to drag the tears from Gudrun. Might I see her unhappy!

"Take Högni and flense him with knife; cut out his heart, make it ready. Fasten grim-minded Gunnar to the gallows. Be bold, have the serpents come."

Högni said: "Do as you wish. I gladly endure it. I prove myself resolute to you, I've been tried before. While we were whole we checked you; now we are wounded, do as you wish."

Then Beiti spoke — he was Atli's steward —: "Let's take Hjalli, and save Högni; let's cut open the half-wit; he is shaped for death, he has lived too long, called always a good for nothing."

The cauldron keeper was scared, ran the length of the room, whimpered, crept into every corner. He said it was not right to pay for their battles, a sad day to die far from his swine and all the goods he once had.

They took Budli's cook and drew him to the knife. The poor thrall cried out, before he felt the point, to let him have time to manure the yard, to do basest work if they would spare him; happy would Hjalli be if they spared his life.

Högni heard it and spoke for the slave — few would do so — that he might go free: ''It would be easier for me to finish this game; why do we want to hear this shrieking?''

They grasped the hero, there was no choice now for the warriors to let him live longer. Högni laughed and all the sons of men heard him. He knew how to last, he could endure torture.

Gunnar took the harp and touched it with his toes. He struck so skilfully that all gentlewomen wept; men cried who heard it. His song had such power the rafters burst asunder.

Then the heroes died while the day was yet young. They had fulfilled their lives.

Atli thought himself grand, he had overcome them both. He told his noble queen of the evil and reproached her: ''Now it is morning, Gudrun. You have lost your faithful kin. What has passed you shaped yourself.''

''Atli, you are happy to reveal murder, but you will forever repent when you feel what is to come. I can tell you that, unless I die, this treasure will prove evil to you.''

''I cannot deny this, but I see another recourse, easier by half. We had it good together; I will comfort you with slaves, beautiful jewels, snow-white silver, all you yourself desire.''

''Have no faith in that. I shall refuse it. I have refused settlement when the cause was less. I was once thought hard, now I will be so. While Högni lived I could bear anything.

''We were raised in one house, grew up in the groves, played games. Grimhild enriched us with gold and necklaces; you can never console me for my brother's death, nor ever make me think it well.

''Strong men destroy women's happiness. The chess king goes to his knees once his pawns are gone; the tree begins to fall when the roots are cut; now you rule everything here, Atli.''

The king was shallow-minded to believe this. Treachery was clear had he been alert. Gudrun was cunning then and spoke with intent. She let on well, but played with two shields.

She prepared an ale feast in her brother's memory. Atli did the same for his followers.

Talk ceased, the drink was ready. They had a banquet and an uproar. Her heart was hard, she loathed Budli's race and would have huge vengeance on her husband.

She enticed the little ones and placed them by the pillars. The boys grew downcast, but did not cry. They rushed towards their mother's bosom, and asked what she intended to do.

''Ask little that! I mean to kill you. I have long wanted to cure you of old age.''

''Bloody your children as you will; no one can stop you. Once you do it, your anger will have short life.''

She struck at the boys in a rage, cut both their throats—an evil exchange. Atli asked where his boys played; he saw them not.

''I will tell Atli everything that happens; Grimhild's daughter will not hide it. Less joy you will feel, Atli, to know it. You caused great woe when you killed my brothers.

''I sleep little since they fell; I promised you hardship, if you remember, the morning you told me; I remember it well. Now it is evening, and you shall hear thus:

''You have lost your heirs, as you should not have. You used their skulls as ale cups. When I gave you drink, I mixed it with blood.

"I took their hearts and stuck them on spits and served them to you saying they were of calves; you alone ate them and left nothing; greedily you chewed as you tested your molars.

"Now you know of your children—few have endured more—I did my part, and I do not boast of it."

"You are grim, Gudrun, if you can do such, mix my drink with the blood of my sons. You killed your own kin, as you should not have. You have shown me little but evil."

"I even wish to kill you, for I could not do enough evil to such a king. You have done such crimes as no one before you, and you increase them, bringing on your death-feast.

"You shall burn on a pyre after you are stoned. Then you will have earned what awaits you."
"Say such hurts tomorrow. I die more finely to pass to another light."

They sat close, angry with one another, neither happy, trading words of hate. Thoughts of revenge waxed in the Niflung, Högni's son. He thought of a great deed. He let Gudrun know of his hate of Atli.

The torments of Högni came into her mind. She said she would be happy if he were avenged. They struck Atli down a short time later. Högni's son and Gudrun herself slew him.

The noble spoke as he was roused from sleep; he knew from his wounds that a bandage was useless: "Tell me the truth, who kills Budli's son? I have been more than little toyed with. I have no hope of life."

"The daughter of Grimhild will not hide it. I have brought it about that your life runs out, and Högni's son, that your wounds overcome you."

"You murder me, though it is unfitting; ill to betray a friend who trusted you. Reluctantly I left home to ask for you, Gudrun.

"You were a widow of praise, and they called you proud. You do not belie it, now that I feel it. You journeyed to my home, an army of followers too. All was dignity in our behaviour.

"Honours I gave plenty for nobles; there was cattle enough; we lived well with much wealth, and many shared it.

"I paid a handsome marriage fee; you got jewelry, thirty thralls, seven good bondmaids. And there was silver. Such was fitting.

"But you esteemed this nothing while before you lay the land Budli left me. You dug it from beneath me so I had not a part. You made your mother-in-law sit and weep; I've had no full heart since we were man and wife."

"You lie now, Atli, though little I care. If I was seldom easy, you made it worse. Your young brothers fought, discords arose between you. Half went to Hel from your house. What should have been favoured was slighted.

"We were three children, thought stubborn. We left the land and followed Sigurd. We roamed, each steered his own ship, wandered according to fate until we came to the east.

"At first we killed a king and chose from his lands. Warriors came beneath our rule, for they knew fear. We freed from outlawry those we wished and set high those who had not been.

"Dead was the Hun and then our fortunes fell; it was a hard lot to be forced a widow; it was a pain to the quick to come to Atli's. Before I had had a hero, ill was the loss.

"We know that you never came from the Thing to pursue a case, or put down another's; you gave way and never held your own. Let it be."

"You lie now, Gudrun; that little helps anyone's cause. We are all diminished. Act now, Gudrun, out of goodness, for our honour when they carry me out."

"I shall buy a ship and a stained chest. I shall wax well the shroud in which to wrap your body, and think of each need as if we had been faithful."

Atli was then a corpse, and his kinsmen's grief increased. The high-born Gudrun fulfilled what she had promised. She wished for peace, and went to kill herself, but her days were lengthened; she was to die another time.

Fortunate is one who gets such offspring, such wolfish children as Gjuki begot. Their wars will live after in every land, wherever people hear of them.

Gudrun's Inciting

After she had killed Atli, Gudrun went down to the shore and waded out into the water, wishing to drown herself, but she could not sink. the current carried her over the firth to the land of King Jonak, who took her for his wife.

Their sons were named Sörli and Erp and Hamdir. Sigurd's daughter, Swanhild was brought up there, and was given in marriage to King Jörmunrek the Great. There was a man at his court named Bikki. Bikki told the king that his own son, Randver, was planning to run away with Swanhild. The king ordered Randver to be hanged and Swanhild to be trampled to death by horses. When Gudrun heard of this, she spoke to her sons.

A tale of terror I was told lately,
Of great grief and of grim words
Uttered by Gudrun, Gjuki's daughter,
As she urged her three sons on to battle.

"Why do you sit there? Why sleep out your lives
In glad talk? You should grieve, rather.
At Jörmunrek's orders horses have trampled
Your half-sister, Swanhild, to death,
Horses of the Goths, grey, road-tamed,
White and black on the war-road.

"You are very unlike the valiant Gunnar,
Far from the hero that Högni was:
If you had the mood of your mother's brothers
Or the hard heart of the Hun king,
You would take a vow to avenge her death."

Then the great-hearted Hamdir spoke:
"You can hardly mean to praise Högni's deed,
When they woke Sigurd, the sleeping hero:
Your blue-white bedspreads were blood-red,
Your coverlet covered with corpse-gore.

"A bitter revenge for your brothers you will take,
If now, as may be, you murder your sons:
If we all took a vow of vengeance together
For Swanhild's sake, we could slay Jörmunrek.

"Since you have incited this sword-talk,
Bring us the blade of the bold king."

Laughing, Gudrun had gone to her quarters
To bring from the shrine the badge of the king
And his broad byrnie: she brought them to her sons;
The bold ones leaped on to the backs of their horses.

Then the great-hearted Hamdir spoke:
  "Fallen among the Goths is the god-of-spears,
He comes no more to our mother's hall:
Drink, mother, in memory of us,
Your three sons and of Swanhild your daughter."

Weeping, Gudrun, Gjuki's daughter,
Went in great sadness to sit in the hall:
Then she uttered her thoughts aloud,
With tears on her cheeks, she told her woe.

"Three fires I have known and three hearths,
For three husbands a home I have made:
Sigurd alone I loved in my heart,
But my brothers brought bane to the hero.

"A heavier sorrow I never saw or knew,
Yet a greater hurt to my heart it had seemed
When the noble warriors wed me to Atil.

"I summoned the boys in secret to me,
I would not work a cure for my bale
Till I had cut off the head of the Niflungs.

"I ran to the coast, I cursed the Norns,
Would free myself from the fate they allotted:
The waves held me, would not drown me,
Bore me to the beach, obliged to live.

"I was bedded a third time—I thought it wise,
Joined in wedlock to Jonak the king:
I bore him babies, boy-heirs.

"Swanhild sat with her serving-maidens,
My only daughter, my dearest child:
Fair Swanhild sat in my hall
As beautiful to behold as a beam of the sun.

"I endowed her with gold, endowed her with fabrics
Before I gave her to the Goth king.
The hardest of all my hurts was when
Swanhild was murdered by mares' feet,
Her white tresses trampled in the mud.

"The sorest was when the weaponless
Sigurd was slaughtered, asleep in his bed,
The grimmest was when glistening serpents
Plunged their fangs into fierce Gunnar,
The keenest was when they cut out
The beating heart of the brave king.

"I must remember many woes.
Saddle, Sigurd, your swart mare,
Grani the swift, and hasten to me.
No daughter sits here, no son's wife,
To give rich gifts to Gudrun now.

"Remember, Sigurd, all we said to each other
When we both lay in bed together:
We vowed that one would visit the other,
Either you from Hel, or I from this world.

"Pile up, thanes, the pyre of oakwood,
Heap it high under the prince:
Let my baleful breast be burned in the fire,
Till all my miseries are melted away.''

(So that the lives of earls be amended,
And the sorrows of ladies be lessened,
This tale of torments was told.)

The Lay of Hamdir

Gruesome deeds grew on the path,
Joyless elves were heard weeping:
At break of day the bale of men
Is at its worst, all woes and afflictions.

It was not now, it was not yesterday,
But long ago; it has long past;
Few things are older by half than the day
When fierce Gudrun, Gjuki's child,
Urged her sons on to vengeance.

"Remember your sister, Swanhild the white:
Jörmunrek ordered horses to trample her,
Goth horses, grey, road-tamed,
White and black, on the war-road.

"You are the last of the leaders of the folk,
You alone are left; our line is diminished.

"I am all alone like the aspen of the forest,
Friends fall away like fir-boughs,
Delights have vanished like leaves from a tree,
Savaged by fire in a season of drought."

Then the great-hearted Hamdir spoke:
"You can hardly mean to praise Högni's deed.
When they woke Sigurd, the sleeping hero,
You sat on the bed while his slayers laughed.

"Your blue-white bedspreads were
Reddened with death-wounds, woven in blood:
When Sigurd died and you sat beside him,
As Gunnar had wished, it was worse for you."

"You thought to hurt Atli by Erp's murder
And the felling of Eitil, but your hurt was greater:
Let each fulfil the fate of the other
With a wound-biting sword, if he wound not himself."

Then Sörli spoke—he was sage in counsel—
"Long talk will not lessen grief:
I will not bandy words with you, mother,
What can you command that will not make you weep?

"You weep for your brothers, you weep for your sons,
Your near-born kin, caught in deception,
Shall sorrow for us, seated on mares,
Fated to fall in a far-off place."

Eager for vengeance, on Hunnish mares,
They went from the court over wet mountains.

They met on the way a wily man:
"Can the short and brown one be of help?"

The bastard answered he would help them now
As one foot befriends the other.
"How can a foot befriend a foot,
One flesh-grown limb lead the other?"

A short answer Erp gave them:
The brave one sat on the back of a mare:
"It is ill for a hero to help cowards."
They said the bastard was too bold to live.

They drew from scabbards deadly blades,
Tempered edges a troll would delight in,
And laid Erp low in the dust:
Less after that by a third was their strength.

They flounced their cloaks, re-fastened their swords
And rode on in their rich garments.

On they went, met a woeful path,
Beheld Randver, hanging from a gallows,
A wing-cold wolf-tree, west of the burg,
Crawling with crane's bait, a cruel sight.

Ale-happy heroes in the hall were merry,
The Goth host: they heard nothing
Till the brave warrior blew his horn.

They cried out to King Jörmunrek,
That helmeted warriors had been sighted;
"King, take counsel; they come for vengeance,
You killed the sister of uncowardly men."

The stout-hearted king stroked his beard,
And laughed grimly, aggressive from wine;
He shook his locks, looked at his shield,
 And twirled the golden goblet he held.

"I would think myself happy if I ever saw
Sörli in my hall and Hamdir with him:
I would bind those boys with bow-strings,
Hang on a gallows Gjuki's sons."

(Hrodglöd heard them by the hall door.
Slender-fingered, she spoke to the boys:)
"Your lives are in peril if you pay me no heed.
Two men against ten hundred:
You cannot bind or beat the goths."

There was din in the hall; ale-cups were shattered;
Blood streamed from the breasts of the Goths.

Then the great-hearted Hamdir spoke:
"King Jörmunrek, we have come to your burg,
Two brothers, born to one mother:
Look at your feet, look at your hands,
Already surrounded by raging flames."

Then bellowed the bold king,
Brave in his byrnie, as a bear roars:
"Since spears will not bite them, nor blades wound,
Slay with stones the sons of Jonak."

Then the great-hearted Hamdir spoke:
"It brought ill, brother, when you opened your bag:
Often from that bag came baleful counsel.

"You'd have had a heart, had you ever thought
How much is wanting in witless men.

"His head would be off now, had Erp lived,
Our battle-wolf brother, the battle-groom,
Whom we slew by the way, the war-wolf man:
What spirit urged me to end his life?

"It was not well like wolves to fight,
It was ill to slay each other,
Like the ever-greedy hounds of the Norns,
Born and bred in the waste.

"Over their corpses, like eagles on boughs,
We wave our swords; we have smitten the Goths:
Our fame is undying, though we die soon;
None live through the night when the Norns have spoken."

At the back of the hall, at the hall gable,
Hamdir sank and Sörli fell.

This is known as the old lay of Hamdir.

Part III

The Mythological Poems

The Words of the High One

Young and alone on a long road,
    Once I lost my way:
Rich I felt when I found another;
    Man rejoices in man.

A kind word need not cost much,
    The price of praise can be cheap:
With half a loaf and an empty cup
    I found myself a friend.

Two wooden stakes stood on the plain,
    On them I hung my clothes:
Draped in linen, they looked well-born,
    But, naked, I was a nobody.

Too early to many homes I came,
    Too late, it seemed, to some:
The ale was finished or else unbrewed,
    The unpopular cannot please.

Some would invite me to visit their homes,
    But none thought I needed a meal,
As though I had eaten a whole joint
    Just before with a friend who had two.

The man who stands at a strange threshold,
    Should be cautious before he cross it,
    Glance this way and that:
Who knows beforehand what foes may sit
    Awaiting him in the hall?

Greetings to the host. The guest has arrived.
    In which seat shall he sit?
Rash is he who at unknown doors
    Relies on his good luck.

Fire is needed by the newcomer
    Whose knees are frozen numb;
Meat and clean linen a man needs
    Who has fared across the fells.

Water, too, that he may wash before eating,
    Handcloths and a hearty welcome,
Courteous words, then courteous silence
    That he may tell his tale.

Who travels widely needs his wits about him,
    The stupid should stay at home:
The ignorant man is often laughed at
    When he sits at meat with the sage.

Of his knowledge a man should never boast,
    Rather be sparing of speech
When to his house a wiser comes:
    Seldom do those who are silent
Make mistakes; mother-wit
    Is ever a faithful friend.

A guest should be cautious when he comes to the table,
    And sit in wary silence,
His ears attentive, his eyes alert:
    So he protects himself.

Fortunate is he who is favoured in his lifetime
    With praise and words of wisdom:
Evil counsel is often given
    By those of evil heart.

Blessed is he who in his own lifetime
    Is awarded praise and wit,
For ill-counsel is often given
    By mortal men to each other.

Better gear than good-sense
    A traveller cannot carry,
Better than riches for a wretched man,
    Far from his own home.

Better gear than good-sense
   A traveller cannot carry,
A more tedious burden than too much drink
   A traveller cannot carry.

Less good than belief would have it
   Is mead for the sons of men:
A man knows less the more he drinks,
   Becomes a befuddled fool.

I-forget is the name men give the heron
   Who hovers over the feast:
Fettered I was in his feathers that night,
   When a guest in Gunnlöd's court.

Drunk I got, dead drunk,
   When Fjalar the wise was with me:
Best is the banquet one looks back on after,
   And remembers all that happened.

Silence becomes the son of a prince,
   To be silent but brave in battle:
It befits a man to be merry and glad
   Until the day of his death.

The coward believes he will live forever
   If he holds back in the battle,
But in old age he shall have no peace
   Though spears have spared his limbs.

When he meets friends, the fool gapes,
   Is shy and sheepish at first,
Then he sips his mead and immediately
   All know what an oaf he is.

He who has seen and suffered much,
   And knows the ways of the world,
He who has travelled, can tell what spirit
   Governs the men he meets.

Drink your mead, but in moderation,
    Talk sense or be silent:
No man is called discourteous who goes
    To bed at an early hour.

A gluttonous man who guzzles away
    Brings sorrow on himself:
At the table of the wise he is taunted often,
    Mocked for his bloated belly.

The herd knows its homing time,
    And leaves the grazing ground:
But the glutton never knows how much
    His belly is able to hold.

An ill-tempered, unhappy man
    Ridicules all he hears,
Makes fun of others, refusing always
    To see the faults in himself.

Foolish is he who frets at night,
    And lies awake to worry:
A weary man when morning comes,
    He finds all as bad as before.

The fool thinks that those who laugh
    At him are all his friends,
Unaware when he sits with wiser men
    How ill they speak of him.

The fool thinks that those who laugh
    At him are all his friends:
When he comes to the Thing and calls for support,
    Few spokesmen he finds.

The fool who fancies he is full of wisdom
    While he sits by his hearth at home,
Quickly finds when questioned by others
    That he knows nothing at all.

The ignorant booby had best be silent
  When he moves among other men,
No one will know what a nit-wit he is
  Until he begins to talk;
No one knows less what a nit-wit he is
  Than the man who talks too much.

To ask well, to answer rightly,
  Are the marks of a wise man:
Men must speak of men's deeds,
  What happens may not be hidden.

Wise is he not who is never silent,
  Mouthing meaningless words:
A glib tongue that goes on chattering
  Sings to its own harm.

A man among friends should not mock another:
  Many believe the man
  Who is not questioned to know much
  And so he escapes their scorn.

An early meal a man should take
  Before he visits friends,
Lest, when he gets there, he go hungry,
  Afraid to ask for food.

The fastest friends may fall out
  When they sit at the banquet-board:
It is, and shall be, a shameful thing
  When guest quarrels with guest.

The wise guest has his way of dealing
  With those who taunt him at table:
He smiles through the meal, not seeming to hear
  The twaddle talked by his foes.

The tactful guest will take his leave
  Early, not linger long:
He starts to stink who outstays his welcome
  In a hall that is not his own.

A small hut of one's own is better,
   A man is his master at home:
A couple of goats and a corded roof
   Still are better than begging.

A small hut of one's own is better,
   A man is his master at home:
His heart bleeds in the beggar who must
   Ask at each meal for meat.

A wayfarer should not walk unarmed,
   But have his weapons to hand:
He knows not when he may need a spear,
   Or what menace meet on the road.

No man is so generous he will jib at accepting
   A gift in return for a gift,
No man so rich that it really gives him
   Pain to be repaid.

Once he has won wealth enough,
   A man should not crave for more:
What he saves for friends, foes may take;
   Hopes are often liars.

With presents friends should please each other,
   With a shield or a costly coat:
Mutual giving makes for friendship
   So long as life goes well.

A man should be loyal through life to friends,
   To them and to friends of theirs,
But never shall a man make offer
   Of friendship to his foes.

A man should be loyal through life to friends,
   And return gift for gift,
Laugh when they laugh, but with lies repay
   A false foe who lies.

If you find a friend you fully trust
    And wish for his good-will,
Exchange thoughts, exchange gifts,
    Go often to his house.

If you deal with another you don't trust
    But wish for his good-will,
Be fair in speech but false in thought
    And give him lie for lie.

Even with one you ill-trust
    And doubt what he means to do,
False words with fair smiles
    May get you the gift you desire.

To a false friend the footpath winds
    Though his house be on the highway:
To a sure friend there is a short-cut,
    Though he live a long way off.

Hotter than fire among false hearts burns
    Friendship for five days,
But suddenly slackens when the sixth dawns:
    Feeble their friendship then.

The generous and bold have the best lives,
    Are seldom beset by cares,
But the base man sees bogies everywhere,
    And the miser pines for presents.

The young fir that falls and rots
    Having neither needles nor bark,
So is the fate of the friendless man:
    Why should he live long?

Little a sand-grain, little a dew-drop,
    Little the minds of men:
All men are not equal in wisdom,
    The half-wise are everywhere.

It is best for man to be middle-wise,
  Not over cunning and clever:
The fairest life is led by those
  Who are deft at all they do.

It is best for man to be middle-wise,
  Not over cunning and clever:
No man is able to know his future,
  So let him sleep in peace.

It is best for man to be middle-wise,
  Not over cunning and clever:
The learned man whose lore is deep
  Is seldom happy at heart.

Brand kindles brand till they burn out,
  Flame is quickened by flame:
One man from another is known by his speech,
  The simpleton by his silence.

Early shall he rise who has designs
  On another's land or life:
His prey escapes the prone wolf,
  The sleeper is seldom victorious.

Early shall he rise who rules few servants,
  And set to work at once:
Much is lost by the late sleeper,
  Wealth is won by the swift.

A man should know how many logs
  And strips of bark from the birch
To stock in autumn, that he may have enough
  Wood for his winter fires.

Washed and fed, one may fare to the Thing
  Though one's clothes be the worse for wear:
None need be ashamed of his shoes or hose,
  Nor of the horse he owns,
    Although no thoroughbred.

As the eagle who comes to the ocean shore,
    Sniffs and hangs her head,
Dumfounded is he who finds at the Thing
    No supporters to plead his case.

It is safe to tell a secret to one,
    Risky to tell it to two,
To tell it to three is thoughtless folly,
    Everyone else will know.

Often words uttered to another
    Have reaped an ill harvest:
Two beat one, the tongue is head's bane,
    Pockets of fur hide fists.

Moderate at council should a man be,
    Not brutal and over-bearing:
Among the bold the bully will find
    Others as bold as he.

These things are thought the best:
    Fire, the sight of the sun,
Good-health with the gift to keep it,
    And a life that avoids vice.

Not all sick men are utterly wretched:
    Some are blessed with sons,
Some with friends, some with riches,
    Some with worthy works.

The halt can manage a horse, the handless a flock,
    The deaf be a doughty fighter,
To be blind is better than to burn on a pyre:
    There is nothing the dead can do.

It is always better to be alive,
    The living can keep a cow:
Fire, I saw, warming a wealthy man,
    With a cold corpse at his door.

A son is a blessing, though born late
   To a father no longer alive:
Stones would seldom stand by the highway
   If sons did not set them there.

He welcomes the night who has enough provisions:
   Short are the sails of a ship,
   Dangerous the dark in autumn,
The wind may veer within five days,
   And many times in a month.

The nit-wit does not know that gold
   Makes apes of many men:
One is rich, one is poor—
   There is no blame in that.

Cattle die, kindred die,
   Every man is mortal:
But the good name never dies
   Of one who has done well.

Cattle die, kindred die,
   Every man is mortal:
But I know one thing that never dies,
   The glory of the great dead.

Fields and flocks had Fitjung's sons,
   Who now carry begging bowls:
Wealth may vanish in the wink of an eye,
   Gold is the falsest of friends.

In the fool who acquires cattle and lands,
   Or wins a woman's love,
His wisdom wanes with his waxing pride,
   He sinks from sense to conceit.

Now is answered what you ask of the runes,
   Graven by the gods,
   Made by the All-mighty,
   Sent by the powerful sage:
It is best for man to remain silent.

For these things give thanks at nightfall:
The day gone, a guttered torch,
A sword tested, the troth of a maid,
Ice crossed, ale drunk.

Hew wood in wind-time, in fine weather sail,
Tell in the night-time tales to housegirls,
For too many eyes are open by day:
From a ship expect speed, from a shield, cover,
Keenness from a sword, but a kiss from a girl.

Drink ale by the hearth, over ice glide,
Buy a stained sword, buy a starving mare
To fatten at home: and fatten the watch-dog.

Trust not an acre early sown,
    Nor praise a son too soon:
Weather rules the acre, wit the son,
    Both are exposed to peril.

A snapping bow, a burning flame,
A grinning wolf, a grunting boar,
A raucous crow, a rootless tree,
A breaking wave, a boiling kettle,
A flying arrow, an ebbing tide,
A coiled adder, the ice of a night,
A bride's bed-talk, a broad sword,
A bear's play, a prince's children,
A witch's welcome, the wit of a slave,
A sick calf, a corpse still fresh,
A brother's killer encountered upon
The highway, a house half-burned,
A racing stallion who has wrenched a leg,
Are never safe: let no man trust them.

                *   *   *

No man should trust a maiden's words,
    Nor what a woman speaks:
Spun on a wheel were women's hearts,
    In their breasts was implanted caprice.

To love a woman whose ways are false
Is like sledding over slippery ice
   With unshod horses out of control,
Badly-trained two-year-olds,
Or drifting rudderless on a rough sea,
Or catching a reindeer with a crippled hand
On a thawing hillside: think not to do it.

Naked I may speak now for I know both:
   Men are treacherous too.
Fairest we speak when falsest we think:
   Many a maid is deceived.

Gallantly shall he speak and gifts bring
   Who wishes for woman's love:
Praise the features of the fair girl,
   Who courts well will conquer.

Never reproach another for his love:
   It happens often enough
That beauty ensnares with desire the wise
   While the foolish remain unmoved.

Never reproach the plight of another,
   For it happens to many men:
Strong desire may stupify heroes,
   Dull the wits of the wise.

The mind alone knows what is near the heart,
   Each is his own judge:
The worst sickness for a wise man
   Is to crave what he cannot enjoy.

So I learned when I sat in the reeds,
   Hoping to have my desire:
Lovely was the flesh of that fair girl,
   But nothing I hoped for happened.

I saw on a bed Billing's daughter,
   Sun-white, asleep:
No greater delight I longed for then
   Than to lie in her lovely arms.

"Come, Odin, after nightfall
   If you wish for a meeting with me:
All would be lost if anyone saw us
   And learned that we were lovers."

Afire with longing, I left her then,
   Deceived by her soft words:
I thought my wooing had won the maid,
   That I would have my way.

After nightfall I hurried back,
   But the warriors were all awake,
Lights were burning, blazing torches:
   So false proved the path.

Towards daybreak back I came.
   The guards were sound asleep:
I found then that the fair woman
   Had tied a bitch to her bed.

Many a girl when one gets to know her
   Proves to be fickle and false:
That treacherous maiden taught me a lesson,
The crafty woman covered me with shame,
   That was all I got from her.

        *   *   *

Let a man with his guests be glad and merry,
   Modest a man should be,
But talk well if he intends to be wise
   And expects praise from men:
Fimbul-fambi is the fool called,
   Unable to open his mouth.

Fruitless my errand, had I been silent
   When I came to Suttung's courts:
With spirited words I spoke to my profit
   In the hall of the aged giant.

Rati had gnawed a narrow passage,
   Chewed a channel through stone,
A path around the roads of giants:
   I was like to lose my head.

Gunnlöd sat me in the golden seat,
   Poured me precious mead:
Ill-reward she had from me for that,
   For her proud and passionate heart,
   Her brooding foreboding spirit.

What I won from her I have well used:
   I have waxed in wisdom since
I came back, bringing to Asgard
   Odrerir, the sacred draught.

Hardly would I have come home alive
   From the garth of the grim troll,
Had Gunnlöd not helped me, the good woman,
   Who wrapped her arms around me.

The following day the Frost-Giants came,
   Walked into Har's hall
   To ask for Har's advice:
Had Bölverk, they asked, come back to his friends
   Or had he been slain by Suttung?

Odin, they said, swore an oath on his ring:
   Who from now on will trust him?
By fraud at the feast he befuddled Suttung
   And brought grief to Gunnlöd.

*   *   *

It is time to sing in the seat of the wise,
  Of what at Urd's Well
I saw in silence, saw and thought on.
  Long I listened to men
(Runes heard spoken, counsels revealed.)
  At Har's hall,
  In Har's hall:
  There I heard this.

Loddfafnir, listen to my counsel:
  You will fare well if you follow it,
  It will help you much if you heed it.

Never rise at night unless you need to spy
  Or to ease yourself in the outhouse.

Shun a woman, wise in magic,
  Her bed and her embraces:
If she cast a spell, you will care no longer
  To meet and speak with men,
Desire no food, desire no pleasure,
  In sorrow fall asleep.

Never seduce another's wife,
  Never make her your mistress.

If you must journey to mountains and firths,
  Take food and fodder with you.

Never open your heart to an evil man
  When fortune does not favour you:
From an evil man, if you make him your friend,
  You will get evil for good.

I saw a warrior wounded fatally
  By the words of an evil woman:
Her cunning tongue caused his death,
  Though what she alleged was a lie.

If you know a friend you can fully trust,
  Go often to his house:
Grass and brambles grow quickly
  Upon the untrodden track.

With a good man it is good to talk,
  Make him your fast friend:
But waste no words on a witless oaf,
  Nor sit with a senseless ape.

Cherish those near you, never be
  The first to break with a friend:
Care eats him who can no longer
  Open his heart to another.

An evil man, if you make him your friend,
  Will give you evil for good:
A good man, if you make him your friend,
  Will praise you in every place.

Affection is mutual when men can open
  All their heart to each other:
He whose words are always fair
  Is untrue and not to be trusted.

Bandy no speech with a bad man:
  Often the better is beaten
  In a word-fight by the worse.

Be not a cobbler nor a carver of shafts,
  Except it be for yourself:
If a shoe fit ill or a shaft be crooked,
  The maker gets curses and kicks.

If aware that another is wicked, say so:
  Make no truce or treaty with foes.

Never share in the shamefully gotten,
  But allow yourself what is lawful.

Never lift your eyes and look up in battle,
Lest the heroes enchant you, who can change warriors
   Suddenly into hogs.

With a good woman, if you wish to enjoy
   Her words and her good-will,
Pledge her fairly and be faithful to it:
   Enjoy the good you are given.

Be not over-wary, but wary enough,
   First, of the foaming ale,
Second, of a woman wed to another,
   Third, of the tricks of thieves.

Mock not the traveller met on the road,
   Nor maliciously laugh at the guest:
Scoff not at guests nor to the gate chase them,
   But relieve the lonely and wretched.

The sitters in the hall seldom know
   The kin of the new-comer:
The best man is marred by faults,
   The worst is not without worth.

Never laugh at the old when they offer counsel,
   Often their words are wise:
From shrivelled skin, from scraggy things
   That hand among the hides
   And move amid the guts,
   Clear words often come.

Heavy the beam above the door;
   Hang a horse-shoe on it
Against ill-luck, lest it should suddenly
   Crash and crush your guests.

Medicines exist against many evils:
Earth against drunkenness, heather against worms,
Oak against costiveness, corn against sorcery,
Spurred rye against rupture, runes against bales,
The moon against feuds, fire against sickness,
   Earth makes harmless the floods.

*   *   *

Wounded I hung on a wind-swept gallows
   For nine long nights,
Pierced by a spear, pledged to Odin,
   Offered, myself to myself:
The wisest know not from whence spring
   The roots of that ancient rood.

They gave me no bread, they gave me no mead:
   I looked down; with a loud cry
I took up runes; from that tree I fell.

Nine lays of power I learned from the famous
   Bölthor, Bestla's father:
He poured me a draught of precious mead,
   Mixed with magic Odrerir.

Learned I grew then, lore-wise,
   Waxed and throve well:
Word from word gave words to me,
Deed from deed gave deeds to me.

Runes you will find, and readable staves,
   Very strong staves,
   Very stout staves,
   Staves that Bölthor stained,
   Made by mighty powers,
   Graven by the prophetic god.

For the gods by Odin, for the elves by Dain,
   By Dvalin, too, for the dwarves,
   By Asvid for the hateful giants,
   And some I carved myself:
Thund, before man was made, scratched them,
Who rose first, fell thereafter.

Know how to cut them, know how to read them,
Know how to stain them, know how to prove them,
Know how to evoke them, know how to sacre them,
Know how to send them, know how to send them.

Better not to ask than to over-pledge
   As a gift that demands a gift,
Better not to send than to slay too many.

The first charm I know is unknown to rulers
   Or any of human kind:
Help it is named, for help it can give
   In hours of sorrow and anguish.

I know a second that the sons of men
   Must learn who wish to be leeches.

I know a third: in the thick of battle,
   If my need be great enough,
It will blunt the edges of enemy swords,
   Their weapons will make no wounds.

I know a fourth: it will free me quickly
   If foes should bind me fast
With strong chains, a chant that makes
   Fetters spring from the feet,
   Bonds burst from the hands.

I know a fifth: no flying arrow,
   Aimed to bring harm to men,
Flies too fast for my fingers to catch it
   And hold it in mid-air.

I know a sixth: it will save me if a man
  Cut runes on a sapling's roots
With intent to harm; it turns the spell;
  The hater is harmed, not me.

I know a seventh: if I see the hall
  Ablaze around my bench-mates,
Though hot the flames, they shall feel nothing,
  If I choose to chant the spell.

I know an eighth: that all are glad of,
  Most useful to men:
If hate fester in the heart of a warrior,
  It will soon calm and cure him.

I know a ninth: when need I have
  To shelter my ship on the flood,
The wind it calms, the waves it smooths
  And puts the sea to sleep.

I know a tenth: if troublesome ghosts
  Ride the rafters aloft,
I can work it so they wander astray,
  Unable to find their forms,
  Unable to find their homes.

I know an eleventh: when I lead to battle
  Old comrades-in-arms,
I have only to chant it behind my shield,
  And unwounded they go to war,
  Unwounded they come from war,
  Unscathed wherever they are.

I know a twelfth: if a tree bear
  A man hanged in a halter,
I can carve and stain strong runes
  That will cause the corpse to speak,
  Reply to whatever I ask.

I know a thirteenth: if I throw a cup
   Of water over a warrior,
He shall not fall in the fiercest battle,
   Nor sink beneath the sword.

I know a fourteenth, that few know:
   If I tell a troop of warriors
About the high ones, elves and gods,
I can name them one by one.
(Few can the nit-wit name.)

I know a fifteenth, that first Thjodrerir
   Sang before Delling's doors,
Giving power to gods, prowess to elves,
Fore-sight to Hroptatyr-Odin.

I know a sixteenth: if I see a girl
   With whom it would please me to play,
I can turn her thoughts, can touch the heart
   Of any white-armed woman.

I know a seventeenth: if I sing it, the young
   Girl will be slow to forsake me.

I know an eighteenth that I never tell
   To maiden or wife of man,
   A secret I hide from all
Except the love who lies in my arms,
   Or else my own sister.

To learn to sing them, Loddfafnir,
   Will take you a long time,
Though helpful they are if you understand them,
   Useful if you use them,
   Needful if you need them.

The Wise One has spoken words in the hall,
   Needful for men to know,
   Unneedful for trolls to know:
Hail to the speaker, hail to the knower,
   Joy to him who has understood,
   Delight to those who have listened.

The Riddles of Gestumblindi

There was a man called Gestumblindi, powerful, but a great enemy of King Heidrek. The king sent word to him to come and make peace if he cared for his life. Gestumblindi was not a wise man; because he knew he could never contend in words with the king, and because he knew the judgement of the king's wise men would be hard on him (for his crimes were considerable), he decided to sacrifice to Odin to ask for help and protection, promising many gifts. One evening there was a knock on his door. Gestumblindi went to the gate and saw a man who had just arrived. He asked his name, and the man called himself *Gestumblindi*, and suggested that they change clothes, and so they did. The man of the house left and the stranger went in where all recognized him as Gestumblindi. The night passed. The next day Gestumblindi went on his way to find the king. He greeted him: the king did not answer. "Lord," he said, "I have come to make peace." The king answered: "Will you submit to the judgement of my wise men?" Gestumblindi asked: "Aren't there other ways to redeem myself?" There are other ways," the king replied, "if you think yourself capable of posing riddles." Gestumblindi said: "I have little ability with that, but the other way seems harder to me." "Will you accept the judgement of my wise men?" "I choose," said Gestumblindi, "to pose riddles." "That is right and proper," said the king, and Gestumblindi began:

> I would have what I had yesterday,
>   —Tell me what that was—
> Overcomer of men, mangler of words,
>   And loosener of loud speech:
> King Heidrek, discover this riddle.
>
>   [Ale]

> From home I went, from home I was going,
>   I saw the way of ways,
> A way below, a way above,
>   And ways every way.
>
>   [Bridge over a river]

What is that drink I drank yesterday,
　It was neither wine nor water,
Mead nor ale, nor any food,
　Yet I went from thence without thirst.

　　　　　　　　　　　　　　[Dew]

Who is the raucous one, who rides hard
　Roads he has ridden before;
Untender is the kiss of his two mouths,
　And on gold alone he goes?

　　　　　　　　　　[Hammer on an anvil]

What is that marvel I met outside
　Before Delling's doors?
Two dead ones had taken a wound-leek
　And boiled it without breath.

　　　　　　　　　　　　[Smith's bellows]

What is the marvel I met outside
　Before Delling's doors?
It has four eyes and eight legs,
　And a belly above its knees.

　　　　　　　　　　　　　　　[Spider]

What is that marvel I met outside
　Before Delling's doors?
Its head is turned toward Hel's road,
　But its feet face the sun.

　　　　　　　　　　　　　　　[Leek]

What is that marvel I met outside
　Before Delling's doors?
Denser than horn, darker than raven,
Whiter than egg-white, no weapon is keener.

　　　　　　　　　　　　　[Obsidian]

Blonde women, two bondmaidens,
Bear to the storehouse some beer-mugs,
Nor hands turn them, nor hammer strikes them,
Erect without are the islands that made them.

　　　　　　　　　　[Female swans and eggs]

Who are the women on the high fell,
　Woman begetting on woman,
Girl on girl begetting a son,
　Though they never knew a man?

[Two angelicas]

I saw the writhing soil-dweller;
　Corpse sat upon corpse.
Blind rode blind on the barge of water,
　The horse had no breath in his body.

[A dead horse on an ice-floe
with a snake on its back]

Who are these thanes? To the Thing they ride
　A bold band of sixteen:
Out they go over the land
　To find a fair home.

[Chessmen]

Who are the women who weaponless fight
　About their liege lord?
All day the dark are on guard,
　But the fair journey forth.

[Hnefatafl, a Nordic
game like backgammon]

Who is it sleeps in the hearth-place,
　Created out of stone?
A lonely orphan, eager for damage,
　There he shall live long.

[Fire from flint]

Who is the great one who goes over earth,
　Devouring water and wood?
He fears no warrior but wind he dreads,
　And his sworn foe is the sun.

[Fog]

What is the creature who kills men's flocks
   And is ringed around with iron.
An eight-horned but headless beast.
   Followed by many fools?

> [*Hunn* in Hnefatafl; (*Hunn* is a pun,
> meaning "bear-cub" as well as
> referring to a piece; the "horns"
> refer to the eight corners of a die)]

What is that beast who wars for the Danes?
Its bloody back is a bulwark to men.
It meets spears, it spares many,
Presses against the palm of man.

> [Shield]

Who are those players who pass over
   The land to their father's delight?
Their hair is pale, their hoods are white,
   And they know nothing of men.

> [Ptarmigans]

Who are those women who weep as they go
   To the joy of their fierce father?
To many men they do mortal harm,
   and will do it as long as they live.

> [Waves]

Who are the maidens, going many together,
   To the fond delight of their father?
Fair-haired, in hoods of white,
   They have never known a man.

> [Waves]

Who are those women who so wildly run
   To the joy of their fierce father?
To the men they meet no mercy they show,
   And are kept awake by the wind.

> [Waves]

Long ago the goose grew big,
Longing for a child, she collected timber:
Swords of straw made a safe home,
Though above stood a bellowing rock.

> [Duck which has built a nest
> in the jaw-bones of an ox]

Who is the great-one who governs many
   And turns himself half towards Hel?
He contends with earth and protects mortals
   If he finds a trusty friend.

> [Anchor]

Who are the women who hurry round the skerries
   Then take a long trip down the firth?
Their bed is hard, their hoods are white,
   And they cannot play in the calm.

> [Waves]

I hailed them in summer at sundown,
   They seemed to me very sad:
The earls were drinking ale in silence,
   But the cask stood there crying out.

> [Piglets sucking a squealing sow]

What is that marvel I met outside
   Before Delling's doors?
It has ten tongues, twenty eyes,
With forty feet sets forth on journeys.

> [Sow with nine piglets]

Four hang and four run,
Two lead and two kick,
One is dirty and dangles after.

> [Cow]

I looked from a sail, I looked on dead men,
Bearing bloody flesh to the bark of a tree.

> [Sitting on a wall seeing a falcon
> carry eider ducks to the crags]

Who are the two with ten feet,
Three eyes, but only one tail?

[Odin on Sleipnir]

What did Odin say in the ear of Baldur
Ere his body was borne to the pyre?

King Heidrek answered: "You alone know that, villain!" Then
Heidrek drew his sword, Tyrfing, and struck at Odin, but Odin
changed into a bird and flew off. The king kept striking at him and
took off his tail-feathers, and that is why the hawk has been short-
tailed ever since.

The Song of Rig

Men say that in the olden days one of the gods, Heimdal, was
walking along a certain sea-shore when he came to a farmhouse
where he called himself Rig.

> Long ago the god Rig
> —Strong he was and wise also—
> Down green ways went striding.
>
> On the middle road Rig came
> To a dwelling-place; the door was ajar.
> A fire was burning on the floor as he entered,
> And by the hearth sat an old couple,
> Ai and Edda, in old-fashioned clothes.
>
> Rig knew how to behave with them:
> He sat down in the centre of the hall
> With the couple of the house on either side.
>
> Then Edda brought a bread-loaf;
> It was unkneaded, heavy and thick,
> Mixed with bran: she brought it to the table,
> Broth in a bowl she brought also,
> And boiled calf, the best of tid-bits.
> Rig rose then, ready for sleep.
>
> Rig knew how to behave with them,
> He chose for himself the centre of the bed,
> With the couple of the house on either side.
>
> There he stayed for three nights,
> Then strode off down the high way:
> For nine months nothing happened.
>
> Then Edda bore a baby with black hair:
> She cleansed him with water and called him Thrall.

Thrall grew and thrived well;
His hands were rough with a wrinkled skin
And his knuckles were gnarled and knotted also;
His face was ugly, his fingers thick,
Hunched his spine, his heels long.

As he grew in strength he began to exert it,
To make boxes, to bind cord,
To carry brushwood back to the house.

A crooked leg came to the yard,
Her soles were muddy, her forearm tanned,
Her nose crooked: she called herself Thir.

She sat down in the centre of the hall,
And the son of the house sat with her;
They chatted much, they made their bed,
Thrall and Thir, for thankless days.

They raised a family and were fairly happy;
Their offspring, I think, were Hreim and Fjosnir,
Klur and Kleggi, Kefsir, Fulnir,
Drumb, Digraldi, Drött and Hösvir,
Lut and Leggjaldi: they laid out the yard,
Manured the fields, fattened the goats,
Tended the swine and tilled the ground.

Their daughters were named Drumba and Kumba,
Ökkvinkalfa and Arinnefja,
Ysja and Ambat, Eikintjasna,
Tötrughypja and Trönubeina:
From thence is descended the Thrall race.

Down the high road Rig was striding,
He came to a dwelling; the door was split;
A fire was burning on the floor as he entered,
And two sat there intent on their work.

The man carved wood for a weaver's beam,
His beard was trimmed, his brown-hair short,
His shirt thonged; a trunk was on the floor.

The woman sat there stretching her arms,
Turning the distaff, a dress-maker;
A snood was on her head, a smock about her chest,
A cloth on her neck, clasps on her shoulders.
To Afi and Amma this house belonged.

Rig knew how to behave with them;
He rose from the table, ready for sleep,
He chose for himself the centre of the bed,
With the couple of the house on either side.

There he stayed for three nights,
Then strode off down the high way:
For nine months nothing happened.

Then Amma bore a baby, bathed him and wrapped him
In clean linen and called him Karl:
He was ruddy of aspect and his eyes squinted.

He grew then and thrived well,
Timbered the house, tamed steers,
Smithied barns, built carts,
Fashioned ploughs and furrows drove.

They came home with Karl's bride,
Carrying keys and clad in goatskins
Snör she was called, she sat under linen:
They kept house together, gave out rings,
Laundered sheets and laboured on the farm.

They raised a family and were fairly happy:
Hal, Thegn and Dreng, Höld and Smith,
Breidur, Bondi, Bundinskeggi,
Bui and Boddi, Brattskegg and Segg.

Their daughters answered to other names,
Snot, Brud, Svanni, Svarri, Sprakki,
Fljod, Sprund and Vif, Feimar, Ristill:
From thence comes the Karl race.

Down the high road Rig was striding,
He came to a dwelling, its doors looked southward,
The gate was open, on the gatepost a ring.

Rig entered: there were rushes on the floor;
He found a couple facing each other
And playing with their fingers, Father and Mother.

On a stool sat the husband; string he twisted,
Bent a bow and burnished arrows:
Thinking of her arms, the housewife sat,
Straightening her sleeves and smoothing linen.

She folded hems, wore fair clasps,
Blue was her blouse and broad her gown,
Her brow was brighter, her breast lighter,
Her neck whiter than the whitest flour.

Rig knew how to behave with them:
He sat down in the centre of the hall
With the couple of the house on either side.

Then Mother appeared with a patterned cloth
Of white linen and laid it on the table,
White-meal bread she brought then,
Thin loaves, and laid them on the cloth.

She set before them full dishes,
Dishes of silver, set on the table
Raw herring and roast fowl;
There was wine in tankards, in tall goblets:
They drank and talked till day was gone.

Rig knew how to behave with them:
Rig rose, readied the bed,
There he stayed for three nights,
Then strode off down the high way:
For nine months nothing happened.

Then Mother bore a baby, bathed him and wrapped him
In silk cloths and called him Jarl.
Blond was his hair, bright his cheeks,
His glance was piercing, a glance like an adder's.

Jarl grew up in the hall and began
To bend bows, to burnish arrows,
To ride horses, let hounds run;
Sounds he swam and swords wielded.

Then from the copse came Rig
To teach him runes; Rig the strider
Named him Rig, named him his son,
Bade him hold ancient dwellings
As his proper fief, the fief that was his.

He rode there through thicket and woods
And holy fells; to a hall he came,
His shield he shook, his spear he brandished.
His horse he spurred, his sword he drew,
He roused to battle, he reddened the fields,
He felled warriors, he won land.

Soon he ruled over eighteen dwellings,
He began to share wealth, to give to all,
Gold and silver and slim-flanked mares,
(Scattered rings and hewed them asunder.)

His messengers went by wet paths,
Came to the hall where Hersir lived;
He had a daughter, Erna by name,
Slender-fingered, fair and wise.

They asked for her hand, then home they drove;
She was Jarl's bride, they bedded together,
Lived at peace and pleased themselves,
Raised a family and were fairly happy.

Bur was the eldest, and Barn the second,
Jod and Adal, Arfi, Mögur,
Nid and Nidjung, Son and Svain;
They played draughts and were doughty swimmers;
One was called Kund, Kon was the youngest.

Jarl's offspring grew up there:
They broke in horses, they bent shields,
Spears they shook and shafts they fixed.

Young Kon learned cunning runes,
Runes eternal and runes mortal,
He learned how he could help men.
(Blunt swords, still seas.)

He knew bird-language, could lessen wounds,
Quench flame and quiet seas;
He had the strength and energy of eight men.

He exchanged runes with Rig-Jarl,
Dealt cunningly with him and became wise;
That is how he earned the right
To be called Rig, the rune-knower.

Kon rode then through thicket and wood,
With his bow-string he stilled birds.

Then a crow said that sat on a branch:
"Why with your string do you still birds?
Rather, Kon, you should ride horses,
Wield swords and slay armies.

"Dan and Danp have dear halls,
A greater heritage than you have now;
Those two know well how to temper edges,
To ride the keel, to cause wounds."

The Sun Song

Grim Greppur brought grief to many,
    Robbed them of riches and life:
No man escaped unscathed who dared
    To walk the roads he watched.

Very often he ate alone,
    Never shared his meat with men,
Till one day a weary stranger
    Sought shelter in his house.

Weak from hunger, weak from thirst,
    That weary traveller was,
But his heart misgave him, for Greppur, he knew
    Had done many evil deeds.

Yet meat and wine to his weary guest
    Greppur willingly gave,
Granted him shelter as God willed,
    Repenting his wicked past.

The thoughts of the other, though, were wicked,
    He rewarded help with harm:
When he rose in the morning he murdered the sleeping
    Good and merciful man.

Greppur cried, "God save me!"
    When he felt the fatal stroke,
And so his sins descended on the man
    Who had killed him without a cause.

Holy angels from Heaven came
    To bear his soul above:
A life of joy he shall live for ever,
    Beholding the Father's face.

*   *   *

No man is ruler of his riches or his health,
  Though often he may be happy:
Ill-luck may befall when least foreseen;
  No man may command his peace.

Never did Unnar, nor Saevaldi,
  Believe that their luck could turn:
Naked they became, nothing was left them,
  They fled as wolves to the woods.

*　　　*　　　*

The power of pleasure had brought pain to many:
  Women often cause harm:
They grow evil, though God the almighty
  Created them pure-in-heart.

Svafadur and Skarthedin were sworn friends,
  Lived their lives for each other;
But the same maiden maddened them both,
  Caused a quarrel between them.

Compared with her beauty no pleasure they took
  In games or the glad daylight:
No other thing could they think about
  Than that bright body of hers.

The dark night became drear to them,
  No longer could they soundly sleep:
Out of such grief there grew a feud
  Between the closest of comrades.

The unpredictable often may
  Have sad and cruel results:
They went to the island for that woman's sake,
  And death was the doom of both.

*　　　*　　　*

Hringvör and Listvör sit in Herdir's doorway,
  Astride Organ's stool:
Drops of iron drip from their nostrils,
  Stirring men to strife.

On the earth-ship rows Odin's wife,
  Inflamed by fleshly lust:
Impure winds puff her sails
  Which are rigged on ropes of passion.

I alone, heir of my father,
  I and Solkötlu's sons
Have read the horn of the hart that wise
  Vigdvalin bore from the barrow.

Read its runes that were roughly scratched
  By the nine daughters of Njörd,
Scored by Krepvör, scored by Bödveig,
  And their other seven sisters.

Svafr and Svafrlögi sucked marrow
  And shed blameless blood:
They dealt in witchcraft and did evil,
  Ever eager to destroy.

               *   *   *

Let no man walk in the ways of pride:
  I can truly testify,
Those who follow them in folly forsake
  The wise ways of God.

Radny and Vebodi were rich and strong,
  Thought none as good as they:
Now in torment they sit, turning their scorched
  Flesh towards the fire.

They trusted in their might, imagined themselves
  All-powerful over others,
But their state presented itself to God
  In a less glorious light.

Many their pleasures, many their delights,
    Gold they enjoyed and girls:
Now they are punished, for in pain they walk
    Between the frost and the flame.

*   *   *

Never put faith in foe's word,
    Though he speak fair before you:
It is good, I say, good to be warned
    By the fate that befalls others.

Sorrow for himself did Sörli get
    When he fell into Vigulf's hands,
And took for truth the treacherous lies
    Of the base who had slain his brother.

He forgave them all from his good heart,
    And they promised to give him gold:
Peace and good-will they pledged together,
    But evil came out of that.

For the next day, the next morning,
    After riding to Rygjardal,
With swords they hewed the innocent one,
    And let his life go forth.

They hauled the corpse by a hidden path,
    And heaved it into a well:
They wished to hide it, but holy God
    Saw all from His heaven.

The just God enjoined his soul
    To abide with Him in bliss:
But his foes are in torment, and the time, I think,
    Will be long before their release.

*   *   *

Ask the disir who do Him service
    To pray that God give you grace:
For a week after all will go
    As well as you could wish.

Do not add to the evil you know
    A deed done in anger,
But comfort grief with good works:
    You will benefit thereby.

Pray to God for good things,
    To Him who made all men:
Great reward shall wise men have
    Who honour the heavenly Father.

A man should pray with especial care
    When he lacks something he longs for:
Nothing asked, nothing given;
    Few notice the needs of the silent.

He called me early, I came late
    To the door of the Wielder-of-doom:
But when He named me, I willed to obey,
    So He won the soul He sought.

Sins rule it so that sadly we journey
    Out of this wonderful world:
None need fear who refrain from evil;
    It is good to be free from guilt.

All faithless hearts to the eye of the Lord
    Are fell as wicked wolves:
After death for ever they shall
    Plod Hel's burning paths.

There are bright virtues that bring wisdom,
    Seven to number and name:
Let your soul love them and forsake them never,
    For in these is health and hope.

       *   *   *

First let me say how I felt happy
    In the abode of bliss:
Second let me say that the sons of men
    Are in dread when they have to die.

Lust and pride and love of riches
   Have turned many men from the truth:
Greed for gold brings grief in the end,
   Money makes apes of many.

I seemed happy to men in many ways,
   Being so blind to evil:
The Lord created the earth we dwell on
   Full of lovely delights.

Long I leaned, long I bent over,
   Much I longed to live:
But God the almighty was more powerful:
   Unfree are the paths of the fated.

I was hard bound in Hel's ropes,
   Sinews about my sides:
Tough they were when I tried to cut them;
   Lucky is he who can loose them.

I found how in all ways affliction swells
   Within my troubled heart:
Much I trembled when Hel's maidens
   Asked me home every night.

I saw the sun, saw how it lightened
   The din-world at dawn:
But heard elsewhere Hel's gates
   Shut with a shuddering clang.

I saw the sun, setting in blood,
   My breath was nigh out of my body:
Mightier it seemed in many ways
   Than it ever had before.

I saw the sun and it seemed to me
   That I looked on the Living God:
I bowed low to it for the last time
   On this Middle-Earth of mortals.

I saw the sun, such was its radiance
    That I seemed to myself in a trance:
But elsewhere ocean roared,
    Mingled with the blood of men.

I saw the sun; at the sight I trembled,
    I was downcast and in dread:
My heart was grieved and greatly troubled:
    My soul was torn asunder.

I saw the sun, so saddened was I
    That my breath was nigh out of my body:
My tongue felt hard as timber and the world
    About me was bitter cold.

I never saw the sun again
    After that downcast day:
The underground waters closed over me then,
    And I turned, cold, from my torments.

Hope fled, so afraid I was,
    Like a bird out of my breast:
High it flew but found nowhere
    A place where it might repose.

Longer than all was that long night
    When I lay stiff on straw:
I grasped then what God had said—
    "Man is made from the dust."

Know and wonder at the works of God
    Who made heaven and earth:
To many their paths are pleasureless,
    Although they forsake sin.

All believe their own works good;
    Rewarded is he who does well.
After wealth what I wish for most
    Is a tomb covered with turf.

*　　*　　*

The lusts of the flesh allure men,
　　Many a soul is enslaved:
Holy water was one of the things
　　Which I had hated most.

For nine days in the Norns' chair
　　I sat, then was set on a horse:
Misshapen suns shone grimly
　　Out of the clouds of the air.

Through the victory-worlds I wished to travel,
　　Through all the seven spheres:
Above and below I looked for a path,
　　A way that would be open.

Now I shall say what I saw first
　　When I entered the realm of Hel:
Souls changed into singed birds
　　Flew in a mass like midges.

Dragons-of-hope flew out of the West
　　And plunged into Glaevald's path,
So wildly they flapped their wings I thought
　　They would split heaven and earth.

Then from the South came the Hart-Sun,
　　Two kept him tame with reins:
On Middle-Earth his hooves stood,
　　But his horns reached to heaven.

Wonderful from the North came the waning moon's
　　Sons—there were seven together:
From brimming horns pure ale they drank
　　At Baugregin's sacred spring.

The wind dropped, the waters calmed,
　　But then there came a great cry
From false women who for foolish men
　　Were milling dust as meat.

Gory stones did those grey women
 Drearily drag along:
Their breasts were torn; their bloody hearts
 Hung out, heavy with sorrow.

Many maimed men I saw,
 Plodding Hel's burning paths:
All reddened were their wretched faces,
 As if bathed in women's blood.

Men trod the dust who had died without
 Receiving the sacrament:
Heathen stars, stained with runes,
 Hung evil over their heads.

Then I saw there those who had envied
 The fair fortune of others:
Their breasts were scored with bloody runes,
 Punishing sin with pain.

Then I saw there those who in life
 Had turned from the paths of truth:
In the after-world the wages for that
 Are to ape the errors of this.

Then I saw there those who had cheated
 Others out of their rights:
They trudged in gangs to Greed City,
 Bearing burdens of lead.

Then I saw there those who had robbed
 Many of money and goods:
Through their breasts, threading their wounds,
 Darted poison-dragons.

Then I looked on those who had least wished
 To observe the sacred days,
Beheld that their hands into hot stone
 Were painfully impaled.

Then I saw there those who from pride
   Looked down with disdain on others:
The garments they wore were woven cunningly
   From fierce undying fire.

Then I saw there those who on earth
   Had been false and faithless in speech :
Out of their heads Hel's ravens
   Without pity pecked their eyes.

There is no end to all the torments
   Sinners suffer in Hell:
For sweet sins sore is the penance,
   Lust is repaid with pain.

       *   *   *

Then I saw there those who had offered
   Gifts to the glory of God:
Holy over their heads stood pure
   Candles burning brightly.

Then I saw there those who had taken
   Pity on the sick and poor:
Over their heads the angels read them
   Gospels and sacred Psalms.

Then I saw there those who had tended
   And fed their father and mother:
Their beds were bathed in the beams of heaven,
   Their couches neatly kept.

Then I saw there those who had often
   Subdued their flesh by fasting:
The angels of the Lord bowed low to them,
   Showing them highest honour.

Then I saw there those who had often
   Laid the scourge to their skin:
Holy maidens had made them clean,
   Washed away their faults.

High in the heavens horses I saw,
    Pacing on paths to God:
The men who rode them had been murdered on earth
    For no crime or cause.

God the Father! God the Son!
    God the Holy Ghost!
Creator of men, I ask you now
    To keep us all from evil.

      *   *   *

You shall recite my song to the living,
    This tale I have told in your ears,
My Sun Song, a song which I think
    Has lied the least to the most.

Part we must now, but shall meet again
    On the final day of doom:
May the God of righteousness give rest to the dead,
    Show mercy to men that live

Skirnir's Ride

Frey, Njörd's son, sat on Hlidskjalf and looked down over the
entire world. He looked north into Gianthome and saw there a
beautiful girl as she went from her father's hall to her bower. That
sight brought great heaviness into his heart. Frey had a servant
called Skirnir. Njörd asked him to discover the cause of Frey's
sadness. Skadi, Njörd's wife said:

> "Arise, Skirnir, ride now
> Swiftly to Frey, my son
> And ask him this: with whom is the wise one
> So angry, so sad at heart."

Skirnir said:

> "A grim answer I shall get, Skadi,
> I fear, from Frey, your son,
> If I ask him this: at whom is the wise one
> So angry, so sad at heart.

> "Tell me, Frey, first of the gods
> That which I long to learn:
> Why do you sit and sulk in your hall
> Alone, my lord, all day?"

> "Why should I tell you what is the cause
> Of the great grief that casts
> Gloom on my mind, though the glory-of-elves
> Lights up the day-time hours."

> "No grief, prince, is so great that you
> May not tell it to me:
> In the days of our youth we were young together,
> Each can trust the other."

> "I saw a girl in Gymir's courts,
> A girl for whose love I long:
> Air and water took on a radiance
> From the light of her lovely arms.

"As dear to no man in days past
  Was maid as she is to me:
But no elf, no god, will grant my prayer
  That I may lie with her."

"Give me a mare that will gallop through
  The wall of flickering flame,
And the sword that slays by itself when battle
  Is joined with the race of giants."

"I will give you a mare that will gallop through
  The wall of flickering flame,
And the sword that slays by itself if brave
  The warrior be who wields it."

Skirnir spoke to his horse:

"Night has fallen: now we must ride
  Over the misty mountains,
The fells of the troll-folk;
We shall both arrive or both fall into
  The hands of the horrible giant."

Skirnir rode into Gianthome and into the garden of Gymir. There
were wild dogs tied by the gate of the yard surrounding the hall of
Gerd. Skirnir rode to where a herdsman sat on a mound and asked
him:

"Hail, herdsman, howe-watcher,
  Looking this way and that!
By what means can I speak, despite his hounds,
  With Gymir's daughter, Gerd?"

"Are you doomed to death, or dead already?
Barred shall you ever be from speech
  With Gymir's daughter, Gerd."

"To stake life on the luck of the dice
  Is better than to be a coward:
The day of my death is destined already,
  By Fate my time is fixed."

Gerd said:

"What is that noise which now I hear,
    That din throughout our halls?
Earth trembles, everything shakes
    In the wide garths of Gymir."

"A man on a mare: he dismounts and leads her
    Unbridled to graze the grass."

"Go, let him in; bid him enter our hall
    And drink a draught of mead,
Though my heart forebodes that my brother's killer
    Darkens the door with his shadow.

"Are you one of the elves, are you one of the gods,
    Or one of the wise Vanes?
Why have you ridden through wild-fire
    Hither to visit our halls?"

"I am not an elf, I am not a god,
    Nor one of the wise Vanes,
Though well I have ridden through wild-fire
    Hither to visit your halls.

"Eleven apples, all of gold,
    Lo, I will give them you, Gerd,
To look on Frey with friendly eyes,
    Call him your dearest dear."

"No, your apples I will never take
    At any wooer's wish,
Nor look on Frey with friendly eyes,
    Nor call him my dearest dear."

"This bracelet I'll give you, that was burned on the
pyre
    Of Baldur, Odin's boy:
It drops eight of equal thickness
    Every ninth night."

"I refuse the bracelet, though burned on the pyre
   Of Baldur, Odin's boy:
I need no gold in Gymir's court;
   His wealth is at my command."

"Do you see this sword, slender, inwrought,
   This sword I hold in my hand?
I will hack your head from your haughty neck
   Unless you pledge your love."

"No threat of force shall frighten me
   To yield to a wooer's wish:
If Gymir, my father, finds you here,
   Short shrift you will get."

"Do you see this sword, slender, inwrought,
   This sword, I hold in my hand?
Beneath its edge will the old one kneel,
   It dooms your father to die.

"With a taming wand I shall teach you swiftly,
   Make you, maiden, obey.
You shall be sent where no son of man
   Or god shall see you again.

"With earth behind you, on an eagle's mound,
   Facing Hel, for ever sit.
Fouler to you shall food look
   Than the snake seems to warriors.

"A sight you shall become ere you come out.
Hrimnir shall leer at you, everyone jeer at you,
   A more famous figure you'll be
Than the god's watchman when you gape through
   the fence.

"May error and terror, blotches and blains,
   Grow on you, grief with tears.
Crouch low while the curse I pronounce,
Heavy torment and two-fold grief.

"Orcs shall pinch you the whole day long
  In the grim garths of the giants,
Every day to the halls of Frost
  You shall creep, crawl without choice,
  Without any hope of choice
Lamentation nor laughter know, day long
  Dejection instead of joy.

"With three-headed trolls shall your time be spent,
  Never shall a man come near you,
May your senses be numbed, your sadness weep,
May you be as the thistle, thoughtlessly crushed
  Underfoot at the gate of the garth.

"To the woods I went, through the wet trees,
  For a spell-binding branch,
  And a fitting branch I found.

"Odin is angry, angry is Thor,
  All the gods shall hate you;
Base maiden, you have brought on yourself
  The anger of all the gods.

"Hear me, giants, hear me frost-trolls,
  Sons of Suttung, hear me,
What I forebode, what I forbid,
  Joy of man to this maid,
  Love of man to this maid.

"Hrimgrimnir shall have you, the hideous troll,
  Beside the doors of the dead,
Under the tree-roots ugly scullions
  Pour you the piss of goats;
Nothing else shall you ever drink,
  Never what you wish,
  Ever what I wish.

"I score troll-runes, then I score three letters,
  Filth, frenzy, lust:
I can score them off as I score them on,
  If I find sufficient cause."

"You have conquered, warrior. This cup I pledge
  you,
  Full of foaming mead,
Little did I dream my love would ever
  Be vowed to a son of the Vanes."

"More must I know for the message I bear
  When I ride from Gymir's garth.
Where will you meet, when will you give
  Yourself to the Son of Njörd?"

"In the woods of Barri which we both know,
  A peaceful, secluded place,
After nine nights to Njörd's Son
  Gerd will give herself."

Then Skirnir rode home. Frey stood outside and greeted him,
asking for news.

"Answer me, Skirnir, ere you dismount
  Or step a foot further:
Is it joyful news from Gianthome
  You bring with you or bad?"

"In the woods of Barri which we both know,
  A peaceful, secluded place,
After nine nights to Njörd's Son
  Gerd will give herself."

"Long is one night, longer are two,
  Endless the thought of three.
Many a month has moved more swiftly
  Than this half of a bridal eve."

The Lay of Harbard

Thor was returning from a journey to the East and came to a sound:
on the other side of the sound was the ferryman with a boat. Thor
cried out:

    Thor   "Who is that fool of fools on the far shore?"

    Harbard   "Who is that clown of clowns who calls across the
            firth?"

    Thor   "Ferry me over: I will feed you this morning.
          In the bag on my back are the best of foods,
          Herrings and goat meat: I am glutted with them.
          Before I left home I ate my fill."

    Harbard   "You would never praise them if you knew all:
          Your kin are mourning; your mother is dead."

    Thor   "What you say is the saddest thing
          A man can hear—that my mother is dead."

    Harbard   "You don't look like a lord with lands of your own:
          Without breeches, bare-footed,
            You look more like a tramp."

    Thor   "Row over your boat and beach it where I show
            you.
          Who owns the boat you hold to the shore?"

    Harbard   "Battle-Wolf: he is wise in counsel
          And sits in a hall on the sound of Radsey .
          I am ordered to refuse horse-thieves and robbers,
          Accept only those I can see are honest:
          Tell me your name if you would travel across."

Thor "I would tell you my name, tell you my lineage,
Were I an outlaw: I am Odin's son,
Meili's brother and Magni's father,
The god who throws. With Thor you deal.
In turn I bid you tell me your name."

Harbard "My name is Harbard: I hide it seldom."

Thor "Why hide your name if not condemned?"

Harbard "Though condemned, unless I be doomed to fall,
I would save my life from such as you."

Thor "Demeaning it would be to wade over
And ruin my gear: you will get what you deserve
For your clodhopper's taunts if I cross the firth."

Harbard "Wade away: I will wait for you.
No harder man have you met since Hrungnir died."

Thor "How dare you refer to my fight with Hrungnir,
The stout-hearted giant with a stone head!
I struck him down; he fell dead before me.
    Meanwhile, what were you doing?"

Harbard "I was with Fjölvar for five winters.
(On the isle named All-green)
We fought battles, felled heroes,
And wooed maidens: we had much to do."

Thor "How were the women you won there?"

Harbard "Lively they were, once they were tamed,
Wise too, once they grew faithful:
Out of sea-sand they spun ropes,
Dug out the bottoms of deep valleys.
Among those fair ones I was first in counsel:
    With seven sisters I dallied
    And had my way with them all.
    Meanwhile, what were you doing?

Thor "The mighty-thewed Thjazi I slew,
   Cast the eyes of the son of All-Wielder
    Up into bright heaven:
   They are the mightiest marks of my works,
   Hereafter to be seen by all mankind.
    Meanwhile, what were you doing?''

Harbard "With potent love-charms I lured from their
husbands
    Hateful night-riding hags:
   A hard giant I thought Hlebard to be;
    He brought me a magic branch,
    But I charmed away his wits.''

Thor "For his good gifts you gave him evil.''

Harbard "One oak gets the fruit that falls from another:
    It is each for himself at all times.
    Meanwhile, what were you doing?''

Thor "I was in the East, the home of the giants,
   And thrashed their brides on their way back to the
fells:
   The giants would rule all, if all were alive,
   All men lie dead under Middle-Earth.
    Meanwhile, what were you doing?''

Harbard "I was in Gaul: I egged on to battle
   Boar-helmets and forbade them peace.
   To Odin belong the earls who are slain,
    But Thor gets the kin of thralls.''

Thor "Unfairly would the gods fare at your hands,
    Were you as strong as you wish.''

Harbard "You are strong enough but not stout-hearted,
   For you cowered, Thor, in the thumb of a glove
    And forgot that you were a god:
   You dared not then, your dread was so great,
   Either sneeze or fart, lest Fjalar hear.''

Thor "Be silent, slave! I would send you to Hel,
Could I but stretch across the firth."

Harbard "Why should you stretch? There is no strife between us.
 Meanwhile, what were you doing?"

Thor "I was in the East, where I held the river:
There the sons of Svarung sought me out,
They lobbed stones but little that helped them,
I beat them down till they begged for peace.
 Meanwhile, what were you doing?"

Harbard "I was travelling in the East where I talked and
 played
With a linen-white one and had a love-meeting:
I gladdened Gold-bright and gave her pleasure."

Thor "You had luck in your choice of a lovely maid."

Harbard "I could have used your help, then, to hold her
fast."

Thor "I would have helped you, had I had the chance."

Harbard "I would have trusted you, had you not betrayed
our pact."

Thor "I am no heel-biter like an old hide-shoe in Spring."

Harbard "Meanwhile, what were you doing?"

Thor "I battled in Hlesey with the Berserk's wives,
Who had done their worst to bewitch the folk."

Harbard "It was base of you, Thor, to battle with women."

Thor "No women they were, but wolves rather:
They shattered my ship on the shore where I
 beached it
And chased away Thjalfi with threatening clubs.
 Meanwhile, what were you doing?"

Harbard "I was with an army; hither we came
To raise banners and redden spears."

Thor "Do you mean that you came to make war?"

Harbard "A ring would better the bargain for you,
A cool umpire to calm our dispute."

Thor "From where did you take such taunting words?
Never have I borne with more bitter taunts."

Harbard "I took them from men, from men of old
Who are housed in Earth's Wood."

Thor "A goodly name you give to barrows
When you hail them as Earth's Wood."

Harbard "Thus I judge such things."

Thor "Little good would you get for your glibness of
tongue
If I should wade through the water:
Louder than a wolf, I believe, you would presently
Howl at a tap from my hammer."

Harbard "You could prove your mettle with more point at
home,
Where Sif in your absence sits with a lover."

Thor "What you say now is of all news the worst:
Shameless coward, I am sure that you lie."

Harbard "I say it is true: you are slow on your journey.
Further would you have stepped had you started at
dawn."

Thor "You lie! It is you who have delayed my journey."

Harbard "I never thought that Thor-of-the-gods
Would be worsted on his way by a herdsman."

| *Thor* | Harbard, bring your boat across now: |
| | Let us argue no more; come to Magni's father." |

| *Harbard* | "Depart from the firth: your passage is denied." |

| *Thor* | "Then show me the way since you won't ferry me." |

Harbard	"Little it is to deny, long it is to travel:
	An hour to the stock, to the stone another,
	Keep left till you reach the Land-of-Man;
	There will Fjörgyn meet Thor, her son,
	And show him the highway to Odin's land."

| *Thor* | "Shall I reach home to-day?" |

| *Harbard* | "With much sorrow and toil by sun-rise |
| | Thor will get home, I think." |

| *Thor* | "We will speak no more: if we meet again, |
| | You shall pay for your refusal to ferry me over." |

| *Harbard* | "Drop dead! May the demons have you!" |

The Lay of Hymir

Long ago the gods had game in abundance,
Ate their fill, feasting together,
Scored runes and relished blood:
In Aegir's hall there was great plenty.

In the hall sat Fell-Dweller, happy as a child,
Much like the kin of Miskurblindi,
Till Ygg's son mockingly met his eye:
"Slave, at our feast you shall serve for ever."

The taunts of the hero troubled the giant,
His thoughts were turned by them to revenge:
"Let Sif's husband bring in the cauldron
That I may brew ale for all the gods."

But none of the gods, none of the powers,
Had such a cauldron; they could not get one.
Until Tyr, the trusty warrior,
Counselled Thunderer with these words.

"Away to the east of Elivagur
At the sky's end wise Hymir lives,
My savage father: he possesses a kettle,
A magic cauldron, miles deep."

Then said Thunderer: "Do you think we can get it?"
"We can," said Tyr, "if cunning enough."

Long they drove, a day's journey
From Asgard, till to Egil they came:
They left their goats to graze with him,
And entered the hall where Hymir lived.

Grandson met grandmother: grim she looked,
A nine-hundred-headed monster:
But white-browed, golden, the wife of Hymir
Brought cups of beer to her son.

"Though you be strong and stout-hearted,
I had better hide you under the cauldron:
Ungenerous with guests is my giant husband,
And very often ill-tempered."

Late to his home came the evil-doer,
Back from the chase; the brutal Hymir
Entered the hall; the icicles clinked
On his chin-forest as the churl came in.

"Now greet, Hymir, with glad mood
Your son who to-night sits in the hall:
He whom we missed has made his way back.
The comrade with him is called Veur,
Hrod's foe and a friend to Man.

Under the gable of the hall they sit,
Protecting themselves with a tall pillar."
The pillar gave at the glance of the giant,
The main beam was broken in pieces.

Eight cauldrons, hard-hammered, fell
One by one from the wood shelf:
They stepped out, but the old giant
Held his foe with a fierce gaze.

Hymir was uneasy, beholding before him
The Peril-of-Giants pacing his floor:
Then at his orders three bulls
Were led away at once to be boiled.

He made each of them a head shorter,
They were carried thence to the cooking-fire.
Before sleeping Sif's husband
Ate two oxen all by himself.

Ample indeed Hrungir's friend
Thought the repast of Thunderer had been:
"If we three are to eat an evening meal
Of game-meat, we must go hunting."

Veur said he was ready to row on the waves
If the villainous giant would provide bait.
"Take your pick of my herd if it pleases you,
Bane-of-Fell-Dwellers, for the bait you need.

There, Veur, I think you will find
Ox-turds easy to get."
Quickly the warrior went to the field
Where, all-black, an ox was grazing.

The Bane-of-Giants broke off
Its two horns from the high place.
"Much worse do I deem your deeds now,
Keel-Wielder, than when you were sitting."

The Goat-Lord bade the Brother-of-Apes
To steer the ship a stretch further,
But the giant was weary, weak already,
And little eager for a longer row.

Fierce Hymir on his fish-hook
Drew up two whales at one cast:
Aft in the stern, Odin's son,
Veur, with patience prepared his line.

With an ox-head his angle he baited,
The slayer of serpents, the saviour of men:
From his hook gaped the gods' foe,
Who under the seas encircles the world.

Doughty Thor drew boldly
The hideous serpent up on board,
Struck with his hammer the high hair-mountain
Of the writhing Coiler, kin-of-the-wolf.

The monster roared, the mountains echoed,
Middle-Earth was mightily shaken,
Then the serpent-fish sank back.

Rueful was the giant as they rowed back,
Far too angry and afraid to speak,
As he laboured to catch a lee wind.

"Now you will have to do half the work,
If I am to get home with my whales
And our sea-buck bring to harbour."

Sif's husband seized the stern
Of the sea-stallion, swung it up
With its bilge-water, oars and bailing-can,
And bore the giant's brim-swine home
Past the boiling springs and the birch-scrub.

Hymir, though, would not own he was beaten,
But continued still to contend with Thor:
"Stoutly you row, but strong you are not
Unless you can break this beaker of mine."

Thunderer took it and threw it quickly
At a stone column that cracked in pieces
And fell down, but the drinking-cup,
When they brought it to Hymir, was undamaged.

Then whispered the beautiful wife of the giant
A secret known to herself alone:
"Harder than the cup is Hymir's skull;
If you want to smash it, smite him there."

The Lord-of-Goats got to his feet,
Exerted every ounce of his strength:
Whole remained Hymir's helmet-stump,
But the wine-cup was cracked in half.

Seeing the shattered shards on his knees,
The giant lamented: "Many good things
Are gone from me, I know; I may never say
From now on—'Ale, be brewed!'

"It is yet to be proved that you can bear
Out of this hall my ale-kettle."
Tyr tried twice to budge it,
But still the cauldron stood where it was.

Sif's husband seized the rim,
His feet broke through the floor of the hall:
He lifted to his head the huge cauldron;
The pot-rings clashed and clattered at his heels.

They had not gone far before he looked
Round behind him: Odin's son
Saw, then, coming from caves in the east,
Hymir with a many-headed throng.

He lifted the kettle, loosed it from his shoulders,
And swung Mjöllnir: he slew all
Those wilderness monsters with his murderous hammer.

They had not gone far before he observed
That Thunderer's goat had gone lame:
The puller-on-the-harness was half dead.
That was malicious Loki's doing.

But you have all heard, all who are skilled
In the lore of the gods, what later happened,
How the waste-dweller was rewarded in return:
Both his sons were the price he paid for that.

The Strong One came to the Council of gods,
Entered with the cauldron Hymir had possessed,
And all the gods from now on could drink
Ale at Aegir's every winter.

Loki's Flyting

Aegir, who was also known as Gymir, had prepared ale for the gods, when he received the great kettle, as was told earlier. To his party came Odin and his wife Frigg. Thor did not come, for he was in the east. Sif, Thor's wife, was there, Bragi and his wife Idun. Tyr was there; he was one-handed; Fenris-wolf had bitten off his hand while being bound. There was Njörd and his wife Skadi, Frey and Freya, and Odin's son Vidar. Loki was there and Frey's servants Byggvir and Beyla. There were many gods and elves. Aegir had two servers, Fimafeng and Eldir. Bright gold served as their fire-light. The ale served itself. There was a great peace in that place, all praised Aegir's servers highly. Loki could not bear to hear praise, so he killed Fimafeng. Then the gods shook their spears at Loki and cried out, driving him away to the woods; then they returned to their drinking. Loki turned back and met Eldir outside. Loki said to him:

> "Stay where you are, step no further,
> Eldir, till you have told me
> Of what the gods, of what the elves,
> Are talking over their ale."

Eldir "They boast of their weapons, their boldness in arms
 As they sit by the banquet-board,
But none of the gods, none of the elves
 Speak of or wish you well."

Loki "I shall go in to eye them feasting
 In Aegir's banquet-hall:
I intend to stir up strife and hate,
 Mingle gall with their mead."

Eldir "If you go in to eye them feasting
 In Aegir's banquet-hall
And sprinkle the gods with spite and malice,
 They will wipe your face with your words."

Loki   "I tell you, Eldir, if we two should begin
        To bandy bitter words,
  I should be ready with apt replies
        Were you to wag your tongue."

Then Loki entered the hall; and when they who were there saw who was before them, they became quiet.

     "From a long journey has Loptur come
        And thirsty is his throat:
     I ask the gods to give me a cup,
        A great goblet of mead.

     "Why so silent and sullen, gods,
        Too moody to speak with me?
     Appoint me a seat, a place at the feast,
        Or else bid me be off."

Bragi   "An appointed seat, a place at the feast,
        The gods will never give you:
  You are not one they wish to invite
        As a friend to their pleasure feast."

Loki   "Remember, Odin, in the olden days
        What blood-brothers we were:
  You would never have dreamed of drinking ale
        Unless it was brought for us both."

Odin   "Make room, Vidar, room for the Wolf's
        Father to sit at our feast,
  Lest Loki abuse us with bitter words
        In Aegir's banquet-hall."

Then Vidar stood and poured for Loki. But before he drank he said to the gods:

Loki   "Hail to the gods, hail to the goddesses,
        Hail to the holy powers,
  Hail to you all, all but one,
        You, Bragi, on that bench."

Bragi "I will give you a mare, a mace also,
      And, to better the bargain, a ring,
  To refrain, Loki, from malicious words,
      Inciting the gods against you."

Loki "Neither horses nor arm-rings have you to give,
      For you lack both, Bragi,
  Of all who sit here, elves and gods,
      The most backward in battle,
  The shyest when arrows are shot."

Bragi "If I were outside, not sitting at table
      In Aegir's banquet-hall,
  My arm would have your head from your neck,
      With pain repay your lies."

Loki "Boldly you speak, less boldly you act,
      Bragi, the bench-ornament:
  If you are angry, come out and fight,
      A hero should feel no fear."

Idun "Think, Bragi, I beg, of our children,
      Of all our kith and kin
  And do not bandy abuse with Loki
      In Aegir's banquet-hall."

Loki "Enough, Idun! I know what you are,
      The most wanton of women:
  Once, half-washed, you wound your arms
      About your brother's killer."

Idun "I will not bandy abuse with Loki
      In Aegir's banquet-hall:
  Be calm, Bragi, and keep the peace,
      Nor let ale rouse you to rage."

Gefjun "Why at the table should two gods
      Bandy bitter words?
  Loki is envious, as we all know,
      And hates the holy powers."

Loki "Enough, Gefjun! I know your secrets,
  I know your seducer's name,
The white god who gave you a jewel
  To lay your leg over his."

Odin "You are mad, Loki, you have lost your wits,
  To give offence to Gefjun:
She is wise, I think, and what is to come
  Beholds as clearly as I."

Loki "Enough, Odin! You have never been.
  A just judge of warriors:
You have often allowed, as allow you should not,
  Faint-hearted fighters to win."

Odin "If I have allowed, as allow I should not,
  Faint-hearted fighters to win,
You lived under the earth for eight winters,
  And bore babies there,
  Were milked like a milch-cow
  And played a woman's part."

Loki "Charms on Samsey, they say you worked,
  Wicked spells like a witch,
Flew about in the form of a wizard
  And played a woman's part."

Frigg "You are mad, Loki, to mention here,
  Aloud among the living,
What befell two gods in former days,
  And disdain their deeds of old."

Loki "Enough, Frigg! You are Fjörgyn's daughter
  And have ever played the whore:
Both Ve and Vili, Vidrir's wife,
  You allowed to lie with you."

Frigg "If I still had a son , sitting here,
  As brave as Baldur was,
You would not escape unscathed from the hall,
  Before you fought with him."

Loki   "If you like, Frigg, there's a lot more
        I can tell you about my tricks:
    For I saw to it that your son died,
        That Baldur will not come back."

Freya   "You are mad, Loki, to mention here
        Your foul and ugly arts:
    Frigg knows all that is fated to be,
        Though she does not say so herself."

Loki   "Enough, Freya! I know well
        You have been as bad as the rest:
    With all who sit here, elves and gods,
        With each you have played the whore."

Freya   "False is your tongue. You will find before long
        That ill comes to the evil:
    The gods are enraged, the goddesses also;
        Unhappy will you go hence."

Loki   "Enough, Freya! I know you a witch
        Who has done many wicked deeds:
    You enticed into bed your own brother, remember,
        And then, Freya, you farted."

Njörd   "It's a small matter if a maiden chooses
        To lie with a husband or lover,
    But a shameful sight is a He-god
        Who has given birth to babies."

Loki   "Beware, Njörd! I know you were sent
        From the east as a hostage to gods:
    For Hrymir's daughters you did as a piss-trough,
        They made water in your mouth."

Njörd   "It comforted me when I came from afar
        In the east as a hostage to gods,
    To beget a son who is greatly loved
        And appears the prince of gods."

Loki   "Beware, Njörd! It is wise to be modest.
        Your secret I shall not conceal:
    On your own sister that son you begot.
        What else would one expect?"

Tyr   "Frey is the best of all bold riders
        In the golden courts of the gods,
    Never dallies with maidens, nor men's wives,
        But frees all from their fetters."

Loki   "Enough, Tyr! You have never known how
        To make peace between men:
    Feeble you are since Fenris bit
        Your right hand off at the wrist."

Tyr   "I lost a hand, but you lost a son,
        The wolf brought woe to us both:
    In painful fetters shall Fenris lie
        Until the twilight of gods."

Loki   "Enough, Tyr! You know that your wife
        Mothered a son by me:
    Nor rag nor penny were you paid for that
        In recompense, wretched one."

Frey   "I see a channel and a chained wolf lying
        Until the twilight of gods:
    Forger of lies, unless you be silent,
        That fate will fall on you next."

Loki   "With gold you bought Gymir's daughter,
        For her you sold your sword:
    When Muspell's sons over Mirkwood ride,
        Faint shall you feel at heart."

Byggvir   "Could I own to the lineage of Ingvi-Frey
        And sit in so honoured a seat,
    I would pound you, crow, to pulp for your words
        And break every one of your bones."

Loki "What do I see wagging its tail
  And yelping like a spoiled pup?
 To Frey it must sound like slave-girls'
  Jibber-jabber at the quern."

Byggvir "My name is Byggvir, known, I think,
  To all for my hot temper:
 Happy am I that Hropt's kin
  Are gathered over their ale."

Loki "Enough, Byggvir! You have never learned
  How to carve meat for men:
 When others fought you hid yourself
  Under the straw of the hall."

Heimdal "Drink, Loki, has dulled your wits,
  It is time to leave it alone:
 When ale begins to take hold of a man,
  He babbles babyish nonsense."

Loki "Enough, Heimdal! I know that fate
  Assigned you a servile task;
 With a damp bottom you are doomed to stay
  Awake to guard the gods."

Skadi "You are lively, Loki, but, like it or not,
  You will not be loose for long:
 The gods will bind you to the blade of a sword
  With the guts of your ice-cold heir."

Loki "If the gods bind me to the blade of a sword
  With the guts of my ice-cold heir,
 I was foremost at the slaughter, first to lay
  Harsh hands on Thjazi."

Skadi "If foremost at the slaughter, first to lay
  Harsh hands on Thjazi,
 Ominous words shall you hear in my temple,
  Dire prophecies on my plains."

Loki   "Livelier your words to Laufey's son
      When you bid him come to your bed:
    Now is the time for telling all,
      That must be told of, too.''

Then Sif came forward and poured foaming mead for Loki, and
said:

    "Hail, Loki! Let me hand you now
      A horn of hoary mead:
    Admit that in one among the gods
      Even you can find no fault.''

He took the horn and drank.

Loki   "That would be Sif, for, wary ever
      And cautious, you kept to yourself,
    Except that you lay with a lover once
      As well as Thor, I think,
      And the lucky one was Loki.''

Beyla   "The fells tremble, the fields shake,
      That must be Thor returning:
    He will surely smite the shameless mocker
      Of gods and the sons of gods.''

Loki   "Enough, Beyla! You are Byggvir's wife
      And mingle in much evil:
    A disgrace it is that where gods sit
      Such a dung-bird and coward should come.''

Then Thor entered and said:

    "Be silent and grovel, of my great hammer
      Mjöllnir shall shut your mouth:
    Your shoulder's stone I will strike from its stem,
      Lifeless you shall lie.''

Loki   "So! The Son-of-Earth is here at last!
     Why do you rant and rage?
  Less bold you will be when you battle with Fenris
     And he swallows Odin whole.''

Thor   "Be silent and grovel, or my great hammer
     Mjöllnir shall shut your mouth:
  Be silent or Thor will throw you to the east
     Where no god shall see you again.''

Loki   "Of your eastward journey, if I were you,
     I would not speak before warriors:
  You cowered, Thor, in the thumb of a glove,
     And forgot that you were a god.''

Thor   "Be silent and grovel, or my great hammer
     Mjöllnir shall shut your mouth:
  My hand will fell you with Hrungnir's-killer,
     Break every one of your bones.''

Loki   "I reckon I shall live to a ripe old age
     For all your threats with the hammer:
  Skrymir's straps were strong, you found,
     When you could not get to your gear
     And almost died of hunger.''

Thor   "Be silent and grovel, or my great hammer
     Mjöllnir shall shut your mouth:
  I will send you to Hel with Hrungnir's-killer,
     Down to the gates of the dead.''

Loki   "I have said to gods and the sons of gods
     What my mind was amused to say:
  But now I shall go, for I know your rages,
     With Thor I'm afraid to fight.

"Ale have you brewed, Aegir, but never
　　Will you give a feast again:
My flames play over all you possess,
　　Already they burn your back."

*　　　　　*　　　　　*

But after that Loki hid in Franang's Falls in the form of a salmon.
There the gods took him. He was bound with the bowels of his son
Nari. But his other son Narfi turned into a wolf. Skadi took a poison
snake and hung it up over the face of Loki; the poison dropped
down. Sigyn, Loki's wife, sat there and held a bowl under the
poison, and when the bowl was full she carried it off; but, meanwhile, the poison dropped on Loki. Then he struggled so hard that
all the earth trembled. We call that now an earthquake.

The Lay of Thrym

The Hurler woke, went wild with rage,
For, suddenly, he missed his sacred Hammer:
He tore his beard, tossed his red locks,
Groped about but could grasp nothing.

Thus, then did Thor speak:
"Loki, Loki, listen well.
Unmarked by man, unmarked by Gods,
Someone has stolen my sacred hammer."

Fast they went to Freya's quarters.
Then said Loki, Laufey's son:
"Freya, will you lend me your feathered cloak
To fly in search of the sacred hammer?"
Freya said:
"I would give it you gladly, were it gold not feathers,
Part with it now, were it pure silver."

Then Loki flew—the feathers whistled—
Out of the door of the hall of gods
On and on to the hall of giants.

There, on a howe, Thrym sat,
Braiding gold collars for his kennel of hounds,
Unteasing the manes of the mares he loved:
Thrym said:
"How fare the gods? How fare the elves?
What brings you on this journey to Gianthome?"

"Ill fare the gods, ill fare the elves.
Have you taken and hidden the hammer of Thunder?"

"I have taken and hidden the hammer of Thunder
Eight miles deep, way under the ground:
Henceforth no god shall get it back
Till you fetch me Freya for my future bride."

Then Loki flew—the feathers whistled—
Out of the door of the hall of giants
On and on to the hall of gods.
Meeting him there in the middle-court,
Thus then did Thor speak:

"Do you come with a message, not mischief only?
Stand where you are. Let me hear your tidings.
He who sits is seldom truthful,
Who stretches at length a liar always."

"I come with a message, not mischief only.
Thrym stole your hammer to hide it away.
Henceforth no god shall get it back
Till we fetch him Freya for his future bride."

Fast they went to Freya's quarters.
Then said Loki, Laufey's son:
"Busk yourself, Freya, in a bridal veil.
You must journey with me to Gianthome."

Freya snorted with fierce rage,
The hall shook and shuddered about them,
Broken to bits was the Brising necklace:
"In the eyes of the gods a whore I should seem,
If I journeyed with you to Gianthome."

The gods hastened to their hall of judgement,
Gathered together, goddesses with them,
Sat in council to consider how
To recover the holy hammer of Thunder.

Heimdal said, sagest of gods,
Who could see the future as his fathers did:
"We must busk Thor in a bridal veil,
Hang about him the Brising necklace,

Bind to his waist a bunch of keys,
Hide his legs in a long dress,
Broad brooches to his breast pin,
With a neat cap cover his locks."

Thus, then, did Thor speak:
"With coarse laughs you will call me a She
If I busk myself in a bridal veil."

Loki replied, Laufey's son:
"Be silent, Thunderer, say no more.
Without the hammer Asgard is lost.
The giants will dwell here, soon drive us out."

They busked Thor then in a bridal veil,
Hung about him the Brising necklace,
Bound to his waist a bunch of keys,
Hid his legs in a long dress,
Broad brooches to his breast pinned,
With a neat cap covered his locks.

Then said Loki, Laufey's son:
"I also shall come as your handmaid with you,
We will journey together to Gianthome."

Quickly the goats were gathered from pasture,
Hurried into harness: eagerly they ran.
Fire scorched the earth, the fells cracked,
As Thunderer journeyed to Gianthome.

Thus, then did Thrym speak:
"Stand up, giants, lay straw on the benches.
They may well bring me my bride now,
Njörd's daughter, from Noatun.

"In my fields there graze gold-horned cattle,
All-black oxen, for my eye's delight.
Much is my treasure, many my gems;
Nothing I lack save lovely Freya."

Evening came: ale and food
Were brought to the benches. The bride quickly
Ate a whole ox and eight salmon,
The sweet dainties reserved for the women,
And more than three measures of mead drank.

Thus, then, did Thrym speak:
"Was ever bride with appetite so keen,
Ever a bride who took such big mouthfuls,
When was more mead drunk by one maid alone?"

Loki, the handmaid, leaning forward,
Found the words to befuddle the giant:
"She has not eaten for eight long nights,
So wild her longing for the wedding-day."

Thrym lifted her veil, leaned to kiss her,
Back he leaped, the full length of the hall:
"How fierce the look in Freya's eyes!
Dangerous the fire that darts out of them."

Loki, the handmaid, leaning forward,
Found the words to befuddle the giant:
"She has had no sleep for eight long nights,
So wild her longing for the wedding-day."

The luckless sister of the luckless giant
Dared to beg for bridal gifts:
"Give me your rings of red gold,
The rings from your fingers, my favour to win,
My good-will, my grace and blessing."

Thus, then, did Thrym speak:
"To bless the Bride now bring the hammer,
Lay Mjöllnir upon the maiden's lap
And wish us joy with joined hands."

Then in his heart Thunderer laughed,
The savage one, when he saw his hammer.
First Thrym he felled to the ground,
Then all his kin he killed in turn.

Laid low his luckless sister
Who had dared to beg for bridal gifts:
Instead of gold she got a blow,
Instead of rings a rap on the skull.

Thus Thor came to recover his hammer.

The Words of the All-Wise

"Bestrew the benches: for my bride and me
  It is time to be turning homeward.
I am eager for this wedding: they are wondering there
  Why I linger so long."

"Of what race are you, White-Nose?
  Were you clasped in the night by a corpse?
I think you must be Thurse-begotten:
  You were never born for a bride."

"All-Wise I am called: under the ground
  I dwell in the dark among stones.
From the Lord-of-chariots I look for good faith:
  It is ill to break an oath."

"I never swore one: I was not at home
  When the gods gave you this pledge.
The bride's father has the best right:
  Permission is for me to give."

"Declare your name, who claim to be
  The father of the fair maid.
Far-wanderer, few know you:
  Whose arm-rings do you wear?"

"The lord Ving-Thor, Longbeard's son,
  Who has travelled wide in the world:
Unless I agree, give my consent,
  You shall never marry the maid."

"You will agree, give your consent
  That I shall marry the maid,
The snow-white woman I desire to have
  Rather than live alone."

"Wise guest, I give you my promise:
　I will not deny you her hand,
If you know what I wish to know concerning
　All the worlds there are.

"Say, Dwarf, for it seems to me
　There is nothing you do not know:
What is earth called, the outstretched land,
　In all the worlds there are?"

"*Earth* by men, *The Fold* by gods,
　Vanes call it *The Ways*,
Giants *Ever-green*, elves *Growing*,
　High gods call it *Clay*."

"What is heaven called, that all know,
　In all the worlds there are?"

"*Heaven* by men, *The Arch* by gods,
　Wind-Weaver by Vanes,
By giants *High-Earth*, by elves *Fair-Roof*,
　By dwarves *The Dripping Hall*."

"What is the moon called, that men see,
　In all the worlds there are?"

"*Moon* by men, *The Ball* by gods,
　The Whirling Wheel in Hel,
The Speeder by giants, *The Bright One* by dwarves,
　By elves *Tally-of-Years*."

"What is sol called, that is seen by men,
　In all the worlds there are?"

"*Sol* by men, *Sun* by gods,
　By dwarves *Dvalin's Doll*,
By giants *Everglow*, by elves *Fair-Wheel*,
　All-Bright by sons of gods."

"What are clouds called, that carry rain,
  In all the worlds there are?"

"*Clouds* by men, *Hope-of-Showers* by gods,
  Wind-Ships by Vanes,
By giants *Drizzle-Hope*, by elves *Weather-Might*,
  In Hel *Helmet-of-Darkness*."

"What is wind called, that widely fares
  In all the worlds there are?"

"*Wind* by men, *Woe-Father* by gods,
  By holy powers *The Neigher*,
The Shouter by giants, *Travelling-Tumult* by elves,
  Squall-Blast they call it in Hel."

"What is calm called, that cannot stir,
  In all the worlds there are?"

"*Calm* by men, *Stillness* by gods,
  Idle-Wind by Vanes,
Over-Warmth by giants, by elves *Day-Quiet*,
  And *Day-Rest* by dwarves."

"What is sea called, that is crossed by men,
  In all the worlds there are?"

"*Sea* by men, *Still-Main* by gods,
  The Vanes call it *Wave*,
Eel-Home by giants, by elves *Water-Charm*,
  The Dark Deep by dwarves."

"What is fire called, so fierce to men,
  In all the worlds there are?"

"*Fire* by men, *Flame* by gods,
  The Flickering One by Vanes,
The Wolfish by giants, *All-Burner* by elves,
  In Hel *The Corpse-Destroyer*."

"What is forest called, that flourishes for men,
  In all the worlds there are?"

"*Forest* by men, *Field's-Mane* by gods,
  By heroes *Mountain Sea-Weed*,
Fire-Wood by giants, *Fair-Bough* by elves,
  By Vanes *Wand-of-Charms*."

"What is night called, that Nör fathered,
  In all the worlds there are?"

"*Night* by men, *The Dark* by gods,
  By holy powers *The Hood*,
Unlight by giants, by elves *Sleep-Pleasure*,
  By dwarves *Spinner-of-Dreams*."

"What is the seed called, that is sown by men,
  In all the worlds there are?"

"*Brew* by men, *Barley* by gods,
  Vanes call it *The Growth*,
Oats by giants, by elves *Water-Charm*,
  In Hel they call it *The Drooping*."

"What is ale called, that is quaffed by men,
  In all the worlds there are?"

"*Ale* by men, *Beer* by gods,
  The Vanes call it *Strength*,
Water-Pure by giants, *Mead* in Hel,
Feast by Suttung's Sons."

"Never have I met such a master of lore
  With such a wealth of wisdom.
I talked to trick you, and tricked you I have:
  Dawn has broken, Dwarf,
  Stiffen now to stone."

The Lay of Vafthrudnir

"Shall I visit Vafthrudnir?
   Afford me your counsel, Frigg:
For I long to meet him and match runes
   In a word-joust with the giant."

"Father-of-warriors, Frigg's counsel
   Is that you stay at home:
No giant is equal, I judge in strength
   And thought to Vafthrudnir."

"Much have I travelled, much have I learned,
   Much have I proved the Powers:
I will venture to visit Vafthrudnir
   And see his hall for myself."

"Unharmed go forth, unharmed return,
   Unharmed back to your own:
May you, Father-of-men, prevail
   In your word-joust with the giant."

So Odin departed to prove the giant,
   Match him wit for wit:
Into the hall of Im's father
   Ygg the fearsome entered.

"Hail, Friend! From afar I have come
   To visit you, Vafthrudnir:
I am eager to learn if you are half-wise
   Or all-wise, as I hear."

"Who are you? Who is it dares
   To toss at me taunting words?
Unless your lore prove larger than mine,
   You shall not leave here alive."

"My name is Gagnrad: now from the road
 I enter your hall in need
Of food and drink; far have I travelled
 For your welcome, wise giant."

"Tell me, Gagnrad, why do you talk from the floor
 And do not seat yourself:
You shall prove to me who has more wit,
 The guest or his old host."

"A poor man among the wealthy
 Must needs speak or be silent:
No good will bragging bring him, I think,
 Who comes to challenge the cunning."

"Tell me, Gagnrad,—you may talk from the floor—
 Tell me to test your boldness:
What is the horse called who hauls forth
 Day for the heroic race?"

"Bright-Mane is he called who the clear day hauls
 Forth for the heroic race:
Mightiest is he thought among the Hreidgoths,
 With his golden-gleaming mane."

"What is the horse called who from the east drags
 Night that seems good to the gods?"

"Ice-Mane is he called who for all drags
 Night that seems good to the gods:
Foam from his bit falls each morning,
 Whence comes dew to the dales."

"What is the river called that runs between
 The grounds of giants and gods?"

"Ifing is the river that runs between
 The grounds of giants and gods:
Open shall it run for evermore
 And never be iced over."

"What is the plain called, the place where Surt
  Shall finally defeat the gods?"

"Vigrid is the plain, the place where Surt
  Shall finally defeat the gods:
A hundred rasts in each direction
  The area is of that plain."

"You are wise, guest: go to the bench,
  Be seated and continue our talk,
To see who in wit is the wiser of us.
  We will stake our heads on the outcome."

"Vouch to me first Vafthrudnir,
  If your wisdom serves you well:
How did the earth, how did the sky,
  Both of them, come to be?"

"From Ymir's flesh was earth shaped,
  The mountains from his mighty bones,
From the skull of Frost-Cold was the sky made,
  The salt sea from his blood."

"Vouch to me second, Vafthrudnir:
Whence comes the moon, whence comes the sun,
  That move alike over men?"

"Mundilferi is the moon's father
  And so of the sun also:
They shall travel through heaven every day
As a tally of times for men."

"Vouch to me third, Vafthrudnir:
Whence comes the day, whence comes the night
  And its moons that fare over men?"

"Delling is the name of Day's father,
  But Night was begotten of Nör,
New Moon and Old were made by the gods
  As a tally of times for men."

"Vouch to me fourth, Vafthrudnir:
Whence came winter and warm summer,
　　How did both of them come to be?"

"Wind-Cold was Winter's father,
　　South the father of Summer."

"Vouch to me fifth, Vafthrudnir:
Whence comes the wind that over waves fares,
　　Unseen by human eyes?"

"Hraesvelg sits at the edge of the world,
　　Huge in eagle feathers:
From his wings, they say, the wind comes
　　That fares over mortal men."

"Vouch to me sixth, Vafthrudnir:
Who of the gods or of Ymir's kin
　　In the First Age was first?"

"In the endless winters before earth was shaped,
　　Then was Bergelmir born:
His father, I think, was Thrudgelmir,
　　As Aurgelmir was his."

"Vouch to me seventh, Vafthrudnir:
Whence did Aurgelmir come who of all the giants
　　In the First Age was first?"

"From Elivagar venom drops
　　Joined to make the giant;
We are all his sons, descended from him,
　　Hence we are all so fierce."

"Vouch to me eighth, Vafthrudnir,
How that grim giant begot children,
　　Who never knew a giantess."

"Under his arm-pits the Ice Giant grew
   A boy and a girl together:
Foot by foot the Fierce One begot
   A six-headed son."

"Vouch to me ninth, Vafthrudnir,
What you first remember, first knew;
   For you know all, do you not?"

"In the endless winters before the earth was shaped,
   Then was Bergelmir born:
What I first remember is the flour bin
   In which they laid the Wise One."

"Vouch to me tenth, Vafthrudnir,
How Njörd comes to be counted a god,
   To have high altars and temples
Raised to his name though not god-born."

"In Vanaheim did the Vanes shape him
   And gave him as pledge to the gods:
After the doom of this age he will return
   Home to the all-wise Vanes."

"Vouch to me eleventh, Vafthrudnir:
Who of the men in Odin's court
   Fare to the fight each day?"

"All the dead warriors in Odin's court
   Fare to the fight each day:
They select the slain, then leave the battle,
   Sit after at peace in the hall."

"Vouch to me twelfth, Vafthrudnir:
From the runes of the giants, from the runes of the
gods,
   Are you able rightly to read
   What fate shall befall the gods?"

"From the runes of the giants, from the runes of the
gods,
   I can read the truth aright:
   I have wandered through all the worlds;
Through the Nine Worlds and through Nether-Hel
   Where die the heroes from Hel."

"Much have I travelled, much have I learned,
   Much have I proved the Powers:
Who will survive when the Arch-Winter
   Shall kill most of mankind?"

"In Hoddmimir's Wood shall be hidden from it
   Lif and Lifthrasir:
For meat they shall feed on morning dew,
   And from both shall men be reborn."

"Whence shall come the Sun to the smooth heaven
   After Fenris has eaten her up?"

"Elf-Candle shall have a daughter
   Before she is seized by Fenris:
The maid shall ride her mother's highway
   When all the High Ones are dead."

"Who are the maids with minds of wisdom
   Who shall glide over the ocean?"

"Maidens in threes over Mögthrasir's
   Village wing their way,
Good spirits who guard homes,
   Although Thurse-begotten."

"Who shall inhabit the home of the gods
   When Surt's flames slacken?"

"Vidar and Vali, the virtuous, shall dwell there,
   When Surt's flames slacken:
To Modi and Magni shall Mjöllnir belong
   When Thor is overthrown."

"By whom in the end shall Odin fall,
   When the High Ones are all destroyed?"

"Fenris will swallow the Father-of-men:
   This will Vidar avenge,
Cleaving asunder the cold jaws
   In the last fight with Fenris."

"What did Odin whisper in the ears of his son
   Before Baldur was borne to the pyre?"

"You alone know that, what long ago
   You said in the ears of your son.
I doomed myself when I dared to tell
   What fate will befall the gods,
And staked my wit against the wit of Odin,
   Ever the wisest of all."

The Lay of Grimnir

King Hraudung had two sons, Agnar and Geirröd. Agnar was ten winters old and Geirröd eight when they went rowing in a boat to catch little fish. But the wind drove them out to sea. During the night they were wrecked on the shore; but they found a peasant with whom they spent the winter. The housewife cared for Agnar and the bondsman cared for Geirröd, teaching him wisdom. In the spring the peasant gave him a boat, and when the couple took the boys to the shore, the peasant spoke to Geirröd in secret. They had a fair wind and came to their father's dock. Geirröd was in the front of the boat. He leapt on to the land and pushed the boat from the shore, saying "Go now where evil may take you!" The boat drifted out to sea. Geirröd went up to the house where he was welcomed, but his father was dead. Then Geirröd was made king and became famous.

Odin and Frigg sat in Hlidskjalf and looked over all the worlds. Odin said, "Do you see Agnar, your foster-child, begetting children with a giantess in a cave? But Geirröd, my foster-child, is a king, ruling over his land." Frigg said, "He is so parsimonious that he tortures his guests if he thinks there are too many of them." Odin replied that this was a great lie; and they wagered about the truth. Frigg sent her maid, Fulla, to Geirröd. She told the king to beware otherwise a magician who had come to the land would bewitch him, and said that he could be recognized because no dog was fierce enough to leap at him. It was a great slander that Geirröd was not hospitable; but he had his men capture the man the dogs would not attack. He wore a dark-blue cloak, called himself Grimnir, and would say no more of himself, even when questioned. The king had him tortured to make him speak, setting him between two fires for eight nights. King Geirröd had a son eight winters old, called Agnar after his father's brother. Agnar went to Grimnir, and gave him a full horn from which to drink, and said that the king was not right in torturing him without cause. Grimnir drank from the horn; the fire was so near that the cloak on Grimnir's back was afire. He said:

"You are fierce, fire, too fierce for comfort,
    Recede from me, savage flame:
My cloak is beginning to catch fire,
    Its fur is singed and smoulders.

"For eight nights I have not moved,
    None offered me meat or mead
Except Agnar: the son of Geirröd
    Shall be lord of the land of the Goths.

"Hail, Agnar! The Highest One
    Bids you a grateful greeting:
For one drink your reward shall be
    Greater than any man got.

"The land is hallowed that lies near
    The homes of gods and elves:
But Thor shall live in Land-of-Strength
    Till the High Ones are all destroyed.

"Ull yonder in Yew-Dale
    Has made himself a mansion:
Elf-Home for Frey in the old days
    The gods gave as a tooth-fee.

"The third is a bower, thatched with silver
    And built by blithe powers:
Hall-of-the-Dead was the home chosen
    Long ago by the god.

"The fourth Sunk-Bench; refreshing waves
    Sparkle and splash about it:
There Odin drinks all day with Saga,
    Glad from golden cups.

"The fifth Glad-Home where, golden-bright
    The hall of Valhalla stands:
There Hropt, the doomer, daily chooses
    Warriors slain by weapons.

"Easy to recognize for all who come there
　Is Odin's lofty hall:
With spear-shafts and shields it is roofed,
　Its benches are strewn with byrnies.

"Easy to recognize for all who come there
　Is Odin's lofty hall:
The wolf hangs before the west door,
　The eagle hovers above.

"The sixth Din-Home, the dwelling once
　Of Thjazi, the mighty-thewed:
Now Skadi sits in the seat of her father,
　The bright bride of gods.

"The seventh Broad-Shining, where Baldur has
　Made himself a mansion,
A blessed place, the best of lands,
　Where evil runes are rare.

"The eighth Heaven-Mount: Heimdal there
　Is lord of land and temple:
The gods' watchman drinks good mead,
　Glad in that peaceful place.

"The ninth Battle-Plain, where bright Freya
　Decides where the warriors shall sit:
Half of the fallen follow the goddess,
　And half belong to Odin.

"The tenth Glittering; it has gold pillars
　And a rich roof of silver:
There Forseti sits as a rule
　And settles every suit.

"The eleventh Harbour, where lordly Njörd
　Has made himself a mansion:
The high-timbered altar he rules,
　Peerless prince of men.

"Vidar lives in the land called Wood,
  Where grass and brushwood grow:
The bold one shall leap from the back of the mare
  To avenge his father's death.

"Sooty-Face in Sooty-with-fire,
  Boils Soot-of-the-Sea:
Boar's flesh to the Battle-slain
  Was ever the finest fare.

"War-accustomed Warrior-Father
  Feeds it to Greedy and Grim,
For on wine alone weapon-good
  Odin always lives.

"Thought and Memory each morning fly
  Over the vast earth:
Thought, I fear, may fail to return,
  But I fear more for Memory.

"Thund roars fiercely, the fish of the wolf
  Frolics in the raging flood:
The river seems too rough and deep
  For the swarm of the slain to wade.

"Gate-of-Dead before doors that are holy
  Stands upon hallowed acres:
Old is that gate, and how to bolt it
  Few now know.

"Five hundred and forty doors
  Are built into Bilskirnir,
Furnished with rings: of roofed halls
  The largest belongs to my son.

"Five hundred and forty doors
  Are built into bright Valhalla:
Eight hundred warriors through one door
  Shall go out to fight with Fenris.

"Heath-Run is the goat in the hall of All-Father
    Who bites at Laerad's boughs:
She shall fill the decanter with clear mead,
    That drink shall never run dry.

"Oak-Thorn the hart in the hall of All-Father
    Who bites at Laerad's boughs:
His horns drip into Hvergelmir,
    Whence all waters rise.

"Sid and Vid, Sökin and Eikin,
Svöl, Fimbulthul, Fjörm and Gunnthro,
    Rinn and Rennandi,
Gipul and Göpul, Gömul and Geirvimul,
    Encircle the hall of the High Ones,
With Thyn and Vin, Thöll and Höll,
    Grad and Gunnthorin.

"Vina is one stream, Vegsvin another,
    A third Thjodnuma,
Nyt and Nöt, Nönn and Hrönn,
Slid and Hrid, Sylg and Ylg,
Vid and Van, Vönd and Strönd,
Gjöll and Leift, they gush down to men
    And afterwards down to Hel.

"Thor shall wade through the waters of Örmt,
    Körmt and the two Kerlaugs,
When he goes each day to deal out fates
    From Yggdrasil the ash-tree.
The bridge of the gods shall burst into flame,
    The sacred waters seethe.

"Glad and Gyllir, Gler, Skeidbrimir,
    Silfrintop and Sinir,
Gisl, Falhofnir, Gulltop, Lettfeti,
    Are the steeds astride which the gods
Ride each day to deal out fates
    From Yggdrasil the ash-tree.

"Three roots spread three ways
    Under the ash Yggdrasil:
Hel is under the first, Frost-Giants under the second,
    Mankind below the last.

"Rat-Tusk is the squirrel who shall run up
    Yggdrasil the ash-tree,
Bearing with him the words of the eagle
    Down to Nidhögg beneath.

"Four the harts who the high boughs
    Gnaw with necks thrown back:
Dain and Dvalin, Duneyr and Durathror.

"Under Yggdrasil hide more serpents
    Than dull apes dream of:
Goin and Moin, Grafvitnir's sons,
    Greyback and Graveruler;
Sleepbringer, Unraveller, shall bite off
    Twigs of that tree for ever.

"The hardships endured by Yggdrasil
    Are more than men can dream of:
Harts bite the twigs, the trunk rots,
    Nidhögg gnaws at the roots.

"My ale-horn is brought me by Hrist and Mist:
    Skeggjöld and Skögul,
Hild and Hlökk, Herfjötur, Thrud,
    Göll and Geirönul,
Rangrid, Radgrid and Reginleif
    Serve ale to the slain.

"Up shall rise All-Swift and Early-Awake,
    Hungry, to haul the sun:
Under their shoulders shall the gods
    Carry cold iron.

"The Cooler he is called who covers the sun
  Like a shield, shining for gods:
Fire would consume fell and ocean
  Should his shield fall.

"Sköll the wolf who shall scare the moon
  Till he flies to the Wood-of-Woe:
Hati the wolf, Hrodvitnir's son
  Who shall pursue the sun.

"From Ymir's flesh was the earth shaped,
  From his blood the salt sea,
The fells from his bones, the forests from his hair,
  The arching sky from his skull;

"From his eyelashes the High Ones made
  Middle-Earth for men,
And out of his brains the ugly-tempered
  Clouds were all carved.

"Ull will grace him, the gods also,
  Who first reaches the flame:
Open to the gods will all worlds be
  When the cauldrons are carried off.

"The sons of Ivaldi ventured of old
  To build Skidbladnir,
The best of ships, for bright Frey,
  The nimble son of Njörd.

"Of all trees is Yggdrasil best,
  Skidbladnir best of ships,
Of gods Odin, of horses Sleipnir,
Bifröst of bridges, Bragi of poets,
Hadbrok of hawks, and of hounds Garm.

"I lift my eyes and look now
  For aid from all the gods,
All the gods who shall enter to sit
  At the benches in Aegir's Hall,
And drink in Aegir's Hall.

"I am called Grim, I am called Traveller
    Warrior and Helmet-Wearer,
Agreeable, Third, Thund and Ud,
    High-One and Hel-Blinder.

"Truth, Change, and Truth-Getter,
    Battle-Glad, Abaser,
Death-Worker, Hider, One-Eye, Fire-Eye,
    Lore-Master, Masked, Deceitful.

"Broad-Hat, Broad-Beard, Boat-Lord, Rider,
All-Father, Death-Father, Father-of-Victory,
But by one name I have never been called
    Since I came among men.

"Masked I am called in the courts of Geirröd,
    But Jalk in Asmund's Hall,
Keeler they say of the sledge-drawer,
    Stirrer-of-Strife at Things,
    Vidur on the field of battle,
Equal-High, Shaker, Shout and Wish,
    Wand-Bearer, Grey-Beard among gods.

"Wise and Sage at Sökkmimir's
    When I hid the old giant:
When I came to Midvitnir's the killer of the Famed
One's
    Son sat there alone.

"You are drunk, dead drunk, Geirröd,
Deprived of reason, deprived of my help,
Of the favour of the fallen, of the favour of Odin.

"I have told you much, you remember too little,
    Friends betray your trust:
Already I see the sword of my friend,
    A blade dripping with blood.

"Soon shall Ygg have your sword-struck corpse,
    Your life's race is run:
Hostile are the incubi, Odin can see,
    Draw on me if you dare.

"I am now Odin, I was Ygg before,
    Thund my name before that,
Wakeful and Heavens-Roar, Hanged and Skilfing,
    Goth and Jalk among gods,
Unraveller, Sleep-Bringer: they are really one,
    Many names for me."

Geirröd sat with his sword on his knee, half drawn from its sheath. When he heard that it was Odin, he rose to take him from the fire. The sword slipped and fell hilt down. The king stumbled and fell and the sword pierced him and slew him. Then Odin vanished, but Agnar ruled there as king for a long time.

Baldur's Dreams

The gods hurried to their hall of council,
Gathered together, goddesses with them,
All-powerful, eager to unriddle
Baldur's dream that such dread portended.

Up rose Odin, unaging magician,
Harnesses Sleipnir, the eight-legged,
Sped down from Heaven to Hel's Deep.

The blood-dabbled hound of Hel faced him,
Howling in frenzy at the father of runes.
The High One halted at the eastern gate,
Where loomed a tumulus, tomb of a witch.
Runes he chanted, charms of power:
Her spectre rose whom his spell commanded
To enlighten the god with the lore of the dead.

"Who is he that on Hel intrudes?
Who calls me up, increasing my grief?
Drenched by hail, driven by storm,
Dew-frozen, I am dead long."

"I am Struggler's Son, Strider, Way-Tamer,
Your secrets I ask: all earth's I know.
Why are Hel's halls hung with jewels,
Her chambers rivers of red gold?"

"For Baldur our mead is brewed strong
In a shining cauldron, a shield over it.
Odin on high in heart despairs.
Unwilling my words: I would no more."

"Far-seeing witch, your words unriddle.
More will I ask: all will I know.
Who shall slay Baldur, best of the gods,
Who suck the life from the son of Odin?"

"Hödur the blind the branch shall throw,
From his brother's body the blood to drain,
Sucking the life from the son of Odin.
Unwilling my words: I would no more."

"Far-seeing witch, your words unriddle.
More will I ask: all will I know.
By whose hand shall Hödur fall
And Baldur's bane be burned with fire?"

"Rindur the blessed shall bring forth Vali.
Though but a night old, he shall be the avenger,
His hands he shall wash not nor his hair comb
Till Baldur's bane is borne to the pyre:
Unwilling my words: I would no more."

"Far-seeing witch, your words unriddle.
More will I ask: all will I know.
Who are the maidens who shall mourn then,
Toss up to heaven their trailing scarves?"

"Way-Tamer you are not, nor are you Strider:
You are Odin the wily, unaging magician."
"Witch you are not, nor woman either:
Womb of monsters, you have mothered three."

"Go home, Odin: air your triumph.
No guest shall again my grave visit,
Till wild Loki tear loose from his bonds
And the World-Wasters on the war-path come."

Song of the Sybil

Heidi men call me when their homes I visit,
A far-seeing witch, wise in talismans,
Caster of spells, cunning in magic,
To wicked women welcome always.

Arm-rings and necklaces, Odin, you gave me
To learn my lore, to learn my magic:
Wider and wider through all worlds I see.

Outside I sat by myself when you came,
Terror of the gods, and gazed in my eyes.
What do you ask of me? Why tempt me?
Odin, I know where your eye is concealed,
Hidden away in the well of Mimir:
Mimir each morning his mead drinks
From Valfather's Pledge. *Well, would you know more?*

Of Heimdal, too, and his horn I know,
Hidden under the holy tree?
Down on it pours a precious stream
From Valfather's Pledge. *Well, would you know more?*

Silence I ask of the sacred folk,
Silence of the kith and kin of Heimdal:
At your will, Valfather, I shall well relate
The old songs of men I remember best.

I tell of giants from times forgotten,
Those who fed me in former days:
Nine worlds I can reckon, nine roots of the tree,
The wonderful ash, way under the ground.

When Ymir lived long ago
Was no sand or sea, no surging waves,
Nowhere was there earth nor heaven above,
But a grinning gap and grass nowhere.

The sons of Bur then built up the lands,
Moulded in magnificence Middle-Earth:
Sun stared from the south on the stones of their hall,
From the ground there sprouted green leeks.

Sun turned from the south, sister of Moon,
Her right arm rested on the rim of Heaven;
She had no inkling where her hall was,
Nor Moon a notion of what might he had,
The planets knew not where their places were.

The high gods gathered in council
In their hall of judgement, all the rulers:
To Night and to Nightfall their names gave,
The Morning they named and the Mid-Day,
Mid-Winter, Mid-Summer, for the assigning of years.

At Ida's Field the Aesir met:
Temple and altar they timbered and raised,
Set up a forge to smithy treasures,
Tongs they fashioned and tools wrought;

Played chess in the court and cheerful were;
Gold they lacked not, the gleaming metal.
Then came three, the Thurse maidens,
Rejoicing in their strength, from Gianthome.

The high gods gathered in council
In their hall of judgement: Who of the dwarves
Should mould man by mastercraft
From Brimir's blood and Blain's limbs?

Motsognir was their mighty ruler,
Greatest of dwarves, and Durin after him :
The dwarves did as Durin directed,
Many man-forms made from the earth.

Nyi and Nidi, Nordri, Sudri,
Austri and Vestri, Althjof, Dvalin,
Bivor, Bavor, Bömbur, Nori,
An and Anar, Ai, Mjödvitnir,
Veigur and Gandalf, Vindalf, Thorin,
Thror and Thrain, Thekkur, Litur,
Vitur, Nar and Nyradur,
Fili, Kili, Fundin, Nali,
Hefti, Vili, Hanar, Sviur,
Billing, Bruni, Bildur, and Buri,
Frar, Hornbori, Fraegur, Loni,
Aurvangur, Jari, Eikinskjaldi:
(All Durin's folk I have duly named.)

I must tell of the dwarves in Dvalin's host;
Like lions they were in Lofar's time:
In Juravale's marsh they made their dwelling,
From their stone hall set out on journeys.

There was Draupnir and Dolgthrasir,
Har, Haugspori, Hlevangur, Gloi,
Dori, Ori, Dufur, Andvari,
Skirvir, Virvir, Skafidur, Ai,
Alf and Yngvi, Eikinskjaldi,
Fjalar and Frosti, Finn and Ginnar:
Men will remember while men live
The long line of Lofar's forbears.

Then from the host three came,
Great, merciful, from the God's home:
Ash and *Elm* on earth they found,
Faint, feeble, with no fate assigned them.

Breath they had not, nor blood nor senses,
Nor language possessed, nor life-hue:
Odin gave them breath, Haenir senses,
Blood and life-hue Lothur gave.

I know an ash-tree, named Yggdrasil:
Sparkling showers are shed on its leaves
That drip dew into the dales below.
By Urd's Well it waves evergreen,
Stands over that still pool,
Near it a bower whence now there come
The Fate Maidens, first Urd,
Skuld second, scorer of runes,
Then Verdandi, third of the Norns:
The laws that determine the lives of men
They fixed forever and their fate sealed.

The first war in the world I well remember,
When Gullveig was spitted on spear-points
And burned in the hall of the high god:
Thrice burned, thrice reborn
Often laid low, she lives yet.

The gods hastened to their hall of judgement,
Sat in council to discover who
Had tainted all the air with corruption
And Odin's maid offered to the giants.

At the host Odin hurled his spear
In the first world-battle; broken was the plankwall
Of the gods' fortress: the fierce Vanes
Caused war to occur in the fields.

The gods hastened to their hall of judgement,
Sat in council to discover who
Had tainted all the air with corruption
And Odin's maid offered to the giants.

One Thor felled in his fierce rage;
Seldom he sits when of such he hears:
Oaths were broken, binding vows,
Solemn agreements sworn between them.

Valkyries I saw, coming from afar,
Eagerly riding to aid the Goths;
Skuld bore one shield, Skögul another,
Gunn, Hild, Göndul and Spearskögul:
Duly have I named the daughters of Odin,
The valiant riders, the valkyries.

Baldur I saw, the bleeding god,
His fate still hidden, Odin's son:
Tall on the plain a plant grew,
A slender marvel, the mistletoe.

From that fair shrub, shot by Hödur,
Flew the fatal dart that felled the god,
But Baldur's brother was born soon after:
Though one night old, Odin's Son
Took a vow to avenge that death.

His hands he washed not nor his hair combed
Till Baldur's bane was borne to the pyre:
Deadly the bow drawn by Vali,
The strong string of stretched gut,
But Frigg wept in Fensalir
For the woe of Valhalla. *Well, would you know more?*

I see one in bonds by the boiling springs;
Like Loki he looks, loathsome to view:
There Sigyn sits, sad by her husband,
In woe by her man. *Well, would you know more?*

From the east through Venom Valley runs
Over jagged rocks the River Gruesome.

North, in Darkdale, stands the dwelling place
Of Sindri's kin, covered with gold;
A hall also in Everfrost,
The banquet hall of Brimir the giant.

A third I see, that no sunlight reaches,
On Dead Man's Shore: the doors face northward,
Through its smoke vent venom drips,
Serpent skins enskein that hall.

Men wade there, tormented by the stream,
Vile murderers, men forsworn,
And artful seducers of other men's wives:
Nidhögg sucks blood from the bodies of the dead,
The wolf rends them. *Well, would you know more?*

In the east dwells a crone, in Ironwood:
The brood of Fenris are bred there,
Wolf-monsters, one of whom
Eventually shall devour the sun.

The giants' watchman, joyful Eggthur,
Sits on his howe and harps well:
The red cock, called All-Knower
Boldly crows from Birdwood.

Goldencomb to the gods crows,
Who wakes the warriors in Valhalla:
A soot-red hen also calls
From Hel's hall, deep under the ground.

Loud howls Garm before Gnipahellir,
Bursting his fetters, Fenris runs:
Further in the future, afar I behold
The twilight of the gods who gave victory.

Brother shall strike brother and both fall,
Sisters' sons defiled with incest;
Evil be on earth, an age of whoredom,
Of sharp sword-play and shields' clashing,
A wind-age, a wolf-age, till the world ruins:
No man to another shall mercy show.

The waters are troubled, the waves surge up:
Announcing now the knell of Fate,
Heimdal winds his horn aloft,
On Hel's road all men tremble.

Yggdrasil trembles, the towering ash
Groans in woe; the wolf is loose:
Odin speaks with the head of Mimir
Before he is swallowed by Surt's kin.

From the east drives Hrym, lifts up his shield,
The squamous serpent squirms with rage,
The great worm with the waves contending,
The pale-beaked eagle pecks at the dead,
Shouting for joy: the ship Naglfar

Sails out from the east, at its helm Loki,
With the children of darkness, the doom-bringers,
Offspring of monsters, allies of the wolf,
All who Byleists's brother follow.

What of the gods? What of the elves?
Gianthome groans, the gods are in council,
The dwarves grieve before their door of stone,
Masters of walls. *Well, would you know more?*

Surt with the bane of branches comes
From the south, on his sword the sun of the Valgods,
Crags topple, the crone falls headlong,
Men tread Hel's road, the Heavens split open.

A further woe falls upon Hlin
As Odin comes forth to fight the wolf;
The killer of Beli battles with Surt:
Now shall fall Frigg's beloved.

Now valiant comes Valfather's son,
Vidar, to vie with Valdyr in battle,
Plunges his sword into the son of Hvedrung,
Avenging his father with a fell thrust.

Now the son of Hlödyn and Odin comes
To fight with Fenris; fiercest of warriors,
He mauls in his rage all Middle-Earth;
Men in fear all flee their homesteads;
Nine paces back steps Bur's son,
Retreats from the worm, of taunts unafraid.

Now death is the portion of doomed men,
Red with blood the buildings of gods,
The sun turns black in the summer after,
Winds whine. *Well, would you know more?*

Earth sinks in the sea, the sun turns black,
Cast down from Heaven are the hot stars,
Fumes reek, into flames burst,
The sky itself is scorched with fire.

I see Earth rising a second time
Out of the foam, fair and green;
Down from the fells, fish to capture,
Wings the eagle; waters flow.

At Ida's Field the Aesir meet:
They remember the worm of Middle-Earth,
Ponder again the great twilight
And the ancient runes of the high god.

Boards shall be found of a beauty to wonder at,
Boards of gold in the grass long after,
The chess-boards they owned in the olden days.

Unsown acres shall harvests bear,
Evil be abolished, Baldur return
And Hropt's hall with Höd rebuild,
Wise gods. *Well, would you know more?*

Haenir shall wield the wand of prophecy,
The sons of two brothers set up their dwelling
In wide Windhome. *Well, would you know more?*

Fairer than sunlight, I see a hall,
A hall thatched with gold in Gimle:
Kind lords shall live there in delight for ever.

Now rides the Strong One to Rainbow Door,
Powerful from heaven, the All-Ruler:
From the depths below a drake comes flying,
The dark dragon from Darkfell,
Bears on his opinions the bodies of men,
Soars overhead. I sink now.

Index of First Lines